Healing the Body of Christ

EMBRACING ABUNDANT LIFE

Avis Sparks PhD

TRILOGY CHRISTIAN PUBLISHERS

TUSTIN, CA

Trilogy Christian Publishers
A Wholly Owned Subsidary of Trinity Broadcasting Network
2442 Michelle Drive
Tustin, CA 92780

For information, address Trilogy Christian Publishing

Rights Department, 2442 Michelle Drive, Tustin, Ca 92780.

Trilogy Christian Publishing/ TBN and colophon are trademarks of Trinity Broadcasting Network.

For information about special discounts for bulk purchases, please contact Trilogy Christian Publishing.

Manufactured in the United States of America

Trilogy Disclaimer: The views and content expressed in this book are those of the author and may not necessarily reflect the views and doctrine of Trilogy Christian Publishing or the Trinity Broadcasting Network.

10 9 8 7 6 5 4 3 2 1

Library of Congress Cataloging-in-Publication Data is available.

ISBN 978-1-64088-573-8

ISBN 978-1-64088-574-5 (ebook)

Contents

Part 4: *Treatment and Prevention*

DEDICATION

I dedicate this work to the family and friends who've nour-
ished and encouraged my spiritual growth. Thank you for
learning, rejoicing, praying, and walking with me.

PREFACE

Healing the Body of Christ addresses the believers' struggle with implementing a lifestyle that promotes a victorious existence in this fallen world. Jesus told us that He came so "that we might have life" (John 10:10), and not just any kind of life, but a full one. So why is the Body of Christ in need of healing? Why are there so many depressed, struggling, negative, backsliding individuals and churches within the community of Christian believers? In John 10:10, Jesus refers to Satan, the adversary of our lives, as a thief who wants to "steal, kill, and destroy." However, Jesus ends by telling us His purpose, which is to give us abundant life. Many Christians are so distracted with the enemy's activities that they are neglecting to receive what Jesus so freely offers: His grace to live a victorious life. Just as we have free will to accept His gift of salvation, we also have free will to yield ourselves to His divine grace. When we abide in His grace, we experience the fullness of life. His grace and Word empower and guide us in not only the spiritual but also the mental, emotional, and physical. We will not address the physical much in this book; however, God is interested in the health of the whole person, not just the spiritual.

The spiritual, mental, and emotional health of the Body of Christ is in jeopardy because many believers have not taken the time to read, understand, and apply the Word of God to their lives. As believers, we place ourselves at an unhealthy disadvantage when we choose to walk in ignorance or rebellion to God's truths. These truths set us free from ideologies and behaviors that trap us in destructive cycles of spiritual, mental, and emotional anguish. The Word of God remedies us of our ignorance so that we will not unknowingly succumb to the ideals and temptation of this world (Hosea 4:6). The Word educates and alerts us to the harmful nature of certain activities, relationships, and mentalities. God wants us whole, healthy, well-informed, and victorious, and we get there through growth. This growth comes from knowing and applying His Word. After we obtain an abundant life and begin growing, He wants us to look beyond ourselves and encourage others within our sphere of influence to seek the Body of Christ.

Healing the Body of Christ is broken up into four parts: "Patient History," "Purpose and Care," "Impediment to Good Health," and "Treatment and Prevention." "Patient History" lays a foundation for understanding the significance and wisdom of the biblical truths discussed in this book about the Body of Christ. Additionally, it provides an overview of humanity's history and relationship with God, Satan, and Christ, and it explains how these relationships affect believers in their endeavor to live healthy, fulfilled, and righteous lives. "Purpose and Care" outlines how God constructed the

Body of Christ to be self-sustaining (supportive, developing, growing, and edifying) in Him when it is maintained, nurtured, and exercised. "Impediments to Good Health" outlines the numerous pitfalls and struggles that believers face when trying to maintain good spiritual, emotional, and mental health. It explores the truths of God, which reveal the snares that hinder the freedom of the believer. Finally, "Treatment and Prevention" reviews the tools, companion (Holy Spirit), and disciplines that Christ instructed us to use toward abundant living.

ACKNOWLEDGEMENTS

God allowed me to mature in understanding and character over the years so that I might write this book. I grew not
only in a scholarly sense but also in experience, gratitude, and
dependence on His grace. I am thankful for His faithfulness,
inspiration, and the words to write this book.

The support of my husband, Kendrick, and his love through
the process of developing this book have been instrumental in
making my dream of publishing this book a reality.

I am blessed to be a mother to our beautiful children, Ellis
and Kensley. They have been instruments of growth in my life
and living expressions of God's love and grace for me.

My mother, Brenda, and brother-in-law, Terrell, took the
time to read through and help me with the unedited versions
of this book, and I am grateful to them.

I also appreciate my sisters, who assisted as sounding
boards while I developed material for the book.

the STRUGGLE

We all struggle at one time or another, and we can perceive it as a failure rather than the progression of life. Struggle shows us that we are learning, growing, and strengthening. We don't like to struggle, so we see it as something negative. The struggle can be perplexing, and we wonder why we have to strive if we were made victorious in Christ. Life can seem overwhelming when we do not see or understand the answers, but we must remember that God is always present to guide and teach us. He has established a path that leads to victory and healing in each of our situations.

As Christian believers, we can struggle to understand and embrace various areas of our faith. We read and hear about the power of God that delivers and heals. We learn lessons and songs about the peace and joy that we can find in Him. However, we don't always see, feel, or experience God's promises in our lives, and this can lead to doubt. We can react to the opposition and conflicts in our lives with frustrations and begin to struggle unrighteously: we regress and pick up old habits and mentalities to help us manage. These once-favorable options of our old nature are now contrary to who we are. We represent the Body of Christ now and must resist using old tactics. Our old ways of handling life do not mirror or follow God's plan for our deliverance and will not result in the abundant life Christ promised.

Righteously struggling is how we embrace abundant life and mature into a healthy version of the Body of Christ. Once saved, we have two competing natures within us: (1) God's Holy Spirit, which calls us to righteousness and relationship with Him, and (2) our old nature, which calls us to rebellion and evil deeds. While on this earth, we must put forth a fighting effort to honor God and establish ourselves in the character and principles of God so that we grow and mature. When successful, we can better resist the call of sin and walk in the nature and love of God.

At times of struggle, we can choose to be frustrated, accept defeat (entering complacency), or become motivated to seek answers. God always offers a solution to our struggles, so we should never settle on frustration or defeat. The answer may not be easy, but it brings healing, deliverance, and growth. Frustration can occur when we try to use our wisdom instead of God's to overcome and succeed. We also feel this frustration when we focus entirely on our agenda instead of nurturing our relationship with God and finding joy in Him as He guides us in our progress. Complacency and defeat can happen when we neglect to practice righteous acts or forget to place our trust in our all-knowing, all-powerful, ever-present God. At different times in my life, I had faith in God's promise but lacked obedience. I possessed a sufficient understanding of God's Word, but I was only applying that which was convenient. I had to realize the truth of 1 Samuel 15:2: "Listen! Obedience is better than sacrifice, and submission is better than offering." My good intentions and actions did not bring me victory in my struggle; however, my obedience to the teachings of God did.

It can be confusing to see believers, whom God called to be conquerors, cycling through bouts of defeat. Some of us can be more stubborn than others at accepting God's answers, but even in our failure to comply, He is there to support us in our growth. In an interview with Minister Steven Furtick, Bishop T. D. Jakes said, "I think sometimes God uses His hand, and sometimes God uses yours. You cannot get God's people out of God's hands, whether they are dysfunctional or emotionally dwarfed." God does not leave or forsake us no matter what our issue is; however, He will allow the consequences of our choices to shape us. We can avoid bad decisions. When we do not, God will use our situations, hurts, and disappointments to direct us toward the right answers for an abundant life through Christ. (All pain and distress are not a result of disobedience.)

When I began to understand that God's promises of healing and living victoriously are parts of a process in a journey of discovery, it became easier to find peace and joy in the everyday. This process contains many different levels, from glory to glory (2 Cor. 3:18). Our advancement through this process and its levels depend on our actions and heart. I truly believe that God does not overstep by taking away our free will. If we do not yield our efforts and hearts, then we hinder Him from moving effectively in our lives. Our failures and struggles do not make God's words a lie. They reveal places of much-needed growth to those who are willing to acknowledge them. At one point in my life, I kept repeating the phrases "I am who I am" or "I am trying," but I felt God tell me I was using these phrases to avoid the tough stuff: growth and maturity. I needed to make a decision. Did I truly want what God had for my life, or would I instead hold on to those excuses? I put that mentality aside and looked at God's Word, which told me who I could become in Christ. I took those words and began my journey with God to grow and mature, addressing those character flaws that hindered me from having victory and peace in every area of my life.

After this revelation, I began working with God in transforming my thoughts and actions to ones that better reflected Him. After this time of growth, life took a downward turn, and instead of getting more relaxed or better, obstacles and disappointments came. I strived to retain an inner peace because of my faith in God, but the world around me seemed bent on chaos. I began to struggle again, even though I had matured and was doing better. Why the discomfort? Why the pain? Then I realized it was time to grow some more. As a part of the Body of Christ, we must grow, and God chose this life as the format in which He will develop us. Get used to the process of the struggle. It is a tool of growth, and it will come and go. However, never get comfortable there. The struggle is there to develop, prepare, and lead us to a more abundant stage of living. We are not to make it a place of residence. So what did I do when I realized what was happening? I huffed and then yielded to the process of becoming a slightly better version of myself—not a perfect version, but one that reflected Christ a little more.

The Blessing of God's Word

God masterfully guided ordinary people, prophets, scholars, and even kings into writing literature that depicts His love, wisdom, grace, plan, and provision for humanity through their life events. The Bible not only commemorates history but also guides us by revealing morals and universal principles that lead to healing, growth, and abundant life. These accounts show how God guides us toward deliverance, maturity, and wholeness. Hopefully, you will see the beauty in the saying "Nothing is new under the sun" and realize just how much wisdom and instruction God's Word provides for us to live life victoriously in the present. As time passes, the fads and governing bodies may change, but God's answers to healing and abundant life remain the same. There are no new viable answers. Abundant life has always begun and only begins with God, for He is the giver of life and Creator of all.

Biblical characters dealt with the same struggles, pains, angst, temptations, and fallibility of humanity that we encounter today. They faced the same types of questions and choices. The Old Testament believers awaited a Savior, whereas we believers, as well as those of the New Testament, walk in the dispensation of grace that Christ established after His death and resurrection. God instructed them to record history so that we can have insight and instruction. The history and words recorded in the Bible hold power (Heb. 4:12) and authority (Ps.

119: 89, 160). The Word of God is there to develop within us the skills we need to live healthy lives and educate us on the tools God uses to transform us and influence the world.

Fighting the Good Fight

Faith is vital to the health of the believer. Faith must be followed by good works to bring life and change (James 2:17). Our faith becomes ineffective in our lives and the lives of others when our hope does not lead us to action. Not until we apply the Word of God will we experience healing and growth: spiritually, mentally, and emotionally. As believers, we must take responsibility for our lives and begin to understand the tools that God gave us to build a healthy and productive life. We must not only understand them but also apply them consistently. Good health comes not from making a few right choices but repeatedly making the right choice. God never promised the church that they wouldn't have to struggle or fight. He declared the exact opposite and told the believer to expect it (John 16:33). Growth and healing require trials and tribulations (James 1:2–4). I am confident that God did not save us so that we could live defeated lives. He wants good things for His children. He wants us to be healthy and whole. However, we must understand that healing and wholeness come in stages. God's work in our lives is a process that conforms us into "the likeness of His Son" (Rom. 8:29) until the day of redemption. This transforming and maturing process is both an individual and community effort, and it requires each believer to do their part and yield to God's wisdom.

> Work hard to show the results of your salvation,
> obeying God with deep reverence and fear. For God is
> working in you, giving you the desire and the power
> to do what pleases him. (Phil. 2:12b–13)

The Body of Christ consists of believers who received the benefits of the works of Christ on the cross. Through His death and resurrection, Christ made available to us His righteousness, an intimate relationship with God, and redemption from sin. The Body of Christ is a part of the kingdom of God and has an eternal and universal role to fulfill. Like most characters in a story, the Body of Christ has an adversary and a problem. The adversary is Satan, and the problem is sin. Sin is a sickness that has corrupted all creation on this earth since Adam and Eve ate from the tree of knowledge of good and evil. The implantation of sin's nature into the consciousness of humanity made us subject to immorality, "for all have sinned and fall short of the glory of God" (Rom. 3:23 NLT). Sin is a sickness that plagues humanity. It separates us from a relationship with God and chains us to a depraved state of being that brings death to the body and soul.

Satan is an enemy to the Body of Christ, but He is not the actual problem. The drug dealer is an obstacle to sobriety for an addict, but the love for the drug is the problem. Our desire for sin is the problem, and it keeps us wandering away from God and sick. The enemy uses sin as a tool to destroy and oppress humanity. Sin is where the struggle of humanity lies. The drug dealer has no power or leverage if there is no desire for the drug.

The same is true with sin; it chains humanity to their vices. Christ's death breaks the chains of sin and delivers the believer from eternal damnation to eternal life, empowering them to live it fully and healthily. Sin no longer has the power to control the believer because they have been reborn with the Spirit of God and freed from sin's shackles. Christ's blood cleanses the believer of unrighteousness and makes them right before God. It also has the power to heal the severe effects of sin. The Holy Spirit guides and renews the believer as they journey through life, helping them avoid the enemy's pitfalls while ministering healing and growth. However, neither Christ's blood nor the Holy Spirit takes away the believer's free will: their ability to listen to the call of sin or indulge in sinful behavior.

Our knowledge and desire for sin do not disappear when we receive salvation. Through salvation, we gain access to the tools and wisdom we need to deal with and overcome sin. As believers, we have the power to denounce sin and reject its call. The Body of Christ consists of redeemed sinners, all of whom are enticed by unrighteous deeds. Sin no longer controls the believer, but it can influence or affect them if the believer allows. Paul speaks of this internal conflict as a struggle between the desire to do God's will and the urges of the flesh to rebel against God's will. We can mature into images of Christ and become more like Him each day.

Salvation brings about a rebirth and makes us new creations. Our inner conflicts occur because we give an audience to old mindsets and behaviors that oppose our new nature. We feel the discomfort of trying to be our former selves in our reborn existence. Mistakes occur, and we have regrets when we use the mentality of our "BC days"—our "Before Christ" days—to approach our life in Christ. He calls us to be holy as He is holy. It sounds daunting; however, holiness only means dedication to God. Holiness calls us toward perfection (Matt. 5:48), which is maturity and growth in God, and we get there through commitment. God said David was a man after His own heart not because he was perfect but because he yielded himself to fulfilling God's purpose (Acts 13:22). David received this title because even though he sinned and had faults, he repented when faced with his transgression and reverence and depended on God for everything. God does not expect perfection but an acknowledgment of our need for Him to handle this life proper and repentance when we falter. We are a member of God's kingdom and are not left to struggle, mature, grow, and figure out what abundant life is by ourselves. We are a part of the Body of Christ, and God does not leave us without support.

More than Conquerors

We can succeed in overcoming the challenges of life, winning the battles within, and defeating the enemy of our soul because God has empowered us to overcome. We do not succeed because we determine it but because God orchestrates it. Victory in the battles of life comes from God. Placing confidence in the wrong person or ability sets us up for defeat and disappointment. When we put faith in our knowledge or another's, we set aside our trust and dependence on God. This misplacement of confidence sets us up for failure. Choosing not to trust in God leads us to not walk in the obedience that makes us conquerors in our everyday life.

By receiving God's love for us, we are more than conquerors, and He will let nothing separate us from Him and all that His love has to offer (Rom. 8:37–39). Before we knew that there was a war, before we began fighting, God had orchestrated our victory. He sent Christ before us to defeat the enemy and then empowered us to win our own individual battles through Christ. Our spiritual triumph of eternal life has not manifested itself fully in our physical lives. Still, as we walk with Christ, we conquer unrighteous mentalities, immoral behavior, and walk-in love.

Christ's work on the cross gives us eternal victory and a secure position as children of God. God has given each of us eternal triumph, but we choose if we walk through our everyday life being conquerors. The first time Moses and the Israelites were at the door of the promised land, they refused to trust God to enable them to defeat the giants and obstacles needed to be victorious. They allowed their fears and faithlessness to overtake them, and they continued to roam the wilderness rather than walk in the promise (Num. 13–14). As believers, we must not allow the enormity of our struggle to cause us to turn our backs on the promises of God. If we want to be victorious, we have to learn to trust in God and place our confidence in His ability to empower us to overcome. We should not settle for sickness, pain, and bondage when God has given us healing and victory for our spirit, mind, and emotions.

When the Israelites made their great exodus out of Egypt, God took them the long route because He knew they were not ready to face the challenges of the Philistines to enter into the promise land (Exod. 13:17). To prepare them for these challenges, God led them through a path of obstacles so they could learn to trust Him and grow in their faith and discipline. But they were like some of us today: they found comfort in their weaknesses, ideals, and anxieties. Instead of building trust and walking in obedience, they stayed doubtful, disobedient, and unsatisfied. When met with opportunities for victory and healing, they returned to old ideals. They accepted defeat and sickness rather than trusting in God. Just as God used the experiences and struggles to teach the Israelites about Him and transform them, He does the same with us. If we submit to His teaching style and learn, we will become more refined and empowered to live this life righteously, experiencing the promises of God.

Overcoming our struggles, tests, and trials on this earth does not qualify us for eternal victory. Christ's work on the cross accomplished that; however, it does contribute to us living an abundant life now. The circumstances and issues that believers experience reveal who we are and then establish who we can become in Christ. While in the wilderness, God showed the Israelites His power and faithfulness, repeatedly teaching those who were willing to learn of His character and love. The second opportunity God gave the Israelites to possess the land, those who grew in faith and trusted God, stood on His Word and readily followed His instructions. They walked around the walls of a fierce enemy, knowing that God would give them victory.

God has a promise for you. Jesus said in Luke 4:18–19, "The Spirit of the Lord is upon me, for he has anointed me to bring Good News to the poor. He has sent me to proclaim that captives will be released that the blind will see, that the oppressed will be set free, and that the time of the Lord's favor has come." Bitterness, rejection, failure, hurt, and addictions can be daunting giants to overcome, but God is bigger than the fight that you face, and He wants to heal and deliver you. God has told us that we are conquerors through Him, and we must learn to trust that. That trust must be followed with obedience so that we can have those victories in our lives. Temptations and challenges will come, but God has given us the tools to overcome and succeed in the face of them. Our struggles help us to acknowledge that we are not alone and have a God on whom we can depend: "The temptations in your life are no different from what others experience. And God is faithful. He will not allow the temptation to be more than you can stand. When you are tempted, he will show you a way out so that you can endure" (1 Cor. 10:13). God wants us to get into the practice of leaning on Him and seeking Him for the wisdom, strength, and grace to overcome. He gives us the breath of life and everything that makes us. We should look to Him as a good father that provides for His children (Acts 17:28). We are God's, and because we are His, we have the responsibility to make good life choices (1 John 4:4). The Spirit of God that lives in us is more significant and higher than the one that operates in the world. Jesus resides in the believer through the Holy Spirit. Death, hell, and the grave will not prevail over the Body of Christ because Christ has already defeated death on our behalf. We have nothing to lose by trusting in God, only a lot to gain.

This book discourages us from becoming complacent and neglecting our responsibility to take care of ourselves. It champions our ability to influence and make a positive difference in our lives and our realm of influence through Christ. Christ came so that we might have abundant life, and this book calls for us to actively walk in it, which means confronting those things in our lives that do not mirror Christ's character. To honestly know when we have achieved abundant life, we must first understand what it is. It is not what the world would depict as abundance. It does not start in material gain, but it can result in it. Abundant life does not begin with prestige or recognition, but it may lead to it. Abundant life is finding contentment in the will, love, and character of God. We can walk in abundant living when our confidence is in God's will and what He provides. Abundant life is cultivating an intimate, healthy relationship with God and humanity. In abundant life, we grow, develop, and become more like Christ.

I studied many cause-and-effect scenarios related to health and disease in the human body and discovered that everything has a source. Everything has a reason and an origin. Our discomfort, ailments, hostile or complacent attitudes, broken relationships, defeatist mentality, or arrogant pride, they all originate from something. God will enlighten us about what is affecting our state of being and give us instructions on how to overcome those things that are keeping us chained. God created all and knows what it will take for us to have health and victory. Let us learn to apply what God has given us and walk in the abundant life offered to us by Christ. As discussed in the next chapter, we must refuse to blindly walk through the cycle of humanity that Adam and Eve have established: rejecting purpose, walking in pride, and reaping the consequences and penalty of sin.

PART 1
Patient History

CYCLE *of* HUMANITY

Most doctor's offices have patients complete a document that provides information about their health history. Among the information requested inChapter   9

clude inquiries about current symptoms, prior illnesses, and diseases that they or their family members may have experienced. This information provides the physician with a history of the individual's health so that they are well informed and have an idea of what may be affecting the patient's condition. After understanding the patient's symptoms and issues, they create a treatment plan. When it comes to our own spiritual, mental, and emotional health, we may not be able to identify all our symptoms or fully understand our history. In this section, "Patient History," we will explore the history of "sin sickness" in humanity, what perpetuates this condition, and how the Great Physician, Jesus, not only heals but also empowers us to walk in wholeness, authority, and abundance. Our spiritual family history reveals to us why we struggle with sin and how our spiritual genetics and environmental factors cause us to battle with the same struggles, temptations, and immorality as our ancestors.

Humanity's Purpose

We must first know our purpose so that we can understand why we struggle and need healing. God created us for relationship. Adam and Eve were created to love and be loved by God. Now we have to be reborn and strive to embrace and fulfill this purpose because of sin sickness. Humanity needs healing because our connection with God, the source of our wellness and health, was damaged. The introduction of the knowledge of sin altered our relationship with Him.

Before we dive into our present circumstances, we must start with the beginning and acknowledge Adam's and Eve's prefall situation so that we can learn from how they went astray. God created Adam and Eve in His image, and He gave them everything they needed to live a good, healthy, purposeful life. He provided all this because of His love for them. He placed them in the garden of Eden to be love and to reciprocate that love. Among all this provision and blessing, God gave them only one restriction: do not eat from the tree of knowledge of good and evil (Gen. 2:8–9). The consequence of disobedience being death. Some people look at Adam's and Eve's situation and immediately acknowledge how blessed they were. God surrounded them with love and provision, giving them one rule that would keep them protected from the knowledge and consequence of sin, a disconnect in humanity's relationship with God.

If we look beyond today's chaos, we can see that God has blessed us in the same manner, providing us purpose and

4

provision. Humanity's situation has changed drastically. Still, God's intention for us stays the same: to love and honor God. Adam's and Eve's act of disobedience, which opened humanity's eyes and hearts to the broad scope of possible evil, leaves us contending with a nature that opposes our purpose. This knowledge tempts us away from embracing God's love for us and constrains us from reciprocating that love through obedience. So yes, we have added opposition; however, God's purpose for us has never changed. In the Gospel of Matthew, Jesus sums up our purpose in the most important commandment: "You must love the Lord your God with all your heart, all your soul, and all your mind" (Matt. 22:37). Humanity's relationship with God is the central theme of our existence, whether we acknowledge it or not. He created us and created all that we know, and He ultimately controls everything in and out of our sphere of existence so that we will look to Him and choose to love and honor Him. He gives us life, resources, skills, opportunities, and relationships and then allows us to define our relationship with Him. It is our choice to embrace our real purpose or not.

God lays out for us not only our purpose in life but also how to fulfill it. In John 14, Jesus shares that we show our love for Him when we keep His Word. He follows that with a promise to send us a comforter, the Holy Spirit, who will teach us and bring God's Word back to our remembrance. The Holy Spirit and God's Word have been given to us so that we can foster an intimate relationship with Him. However, just as Adam and Eve wanted to define themselves by something other than God's Word and His love, humanity wants to do the same today.

We look to find purpose in other relationships, jobs, hobbies, and pursuits, but they are only avenues by which we show our love and faith in God.

Rejecting Purpose

God created Adam and Eve and placed them in a cocoon of His love in the garden of Eden. It provided everything that they needed and was free of death and illness, something we all long to experience today. God also gave them free will. They could choose to stay for eternity in a state of peace and harmony or decide to undergo a depraved state of existence. They chose the latter. God gave Adam and Eve instructions to subdue the earth and procreate and told them not to eat of the tree of knowledge of good and evil. They would have shown their love for God through their obedience. Instead of displaying their love for God, they chose self-exaltation. We see this pattern continuing throughout the history of humanity as if we are genetically predisposed to this condition of sin, and in all actuality, we are. In Paul's epistle to the Romans, he tells us that "when Adam sinned, sin entered the world. Adam's sin brought death, so death spread to everyone, for everyone sinned" (Rom. 5:12). We are born with a nature that rebels against God because of Adam's sin. But even in this state, God loves us. He wants us to walk in our purpose and has given us a way to redemption. Romans 5:8–10 tells us thus:

But God showed his great love for us by sending Christ to die for us while we were still sinners. And

6

since we have been made right in God's sight by the blood of Christ, he will certainly save us from God's condemnation. For since our friendship with God was restored by the death of his Son while we were still his enemies, we will certainly be saved through the life of his Son.

Adam and Eve did not surprise God when they sinned. When He placed them in the garden of Eden, He knew what they were capable of and still created them with free will to determine how they would define themselves and live their lives. He knew that humanity would fall, and He planned for its redemption "long before the world began" (1 Pet. 1:20). We cannot redeem ourselves. We can struggle fervently within ourselves daily and still not be able to declare ourselves righteous. Christ was given as our Redeemer so that we could become right with God (Rom. 10:9) and the Holy Spirit as our helper to guide us into all truth (John 16:13). God provided a way for humanity to have an intimate relationship with Him again, and we simply have to receive the work of Christ on the cross.

God knows us and loves us. He opens His arms, inviting us into relationship through the death of His Son, so that we may live the rest of our lives fulfilling our purpose. Nevertheless, we are continually trying to define who we are so that we can allocate worth to our existence. We mistakenly look to worldly standards to define ourselves, forgetting that God has already established for us a purpose that gives our lives meaning and worth. Our inclination to sin should never cause us to doubt the worth or value God has placed on humanity. Sin taints us; however, it does not take away the beauty of our purpose in the eyesight of God. David wrote in Psalm 139:14, "I praise you because I am fearfully and wonderfully made; your works are wonderful; I know that full well." We should not let society's ideologies and enticements keep us from this truth. God knows and understands the heart of humanity. Psalm 33:13–15 says, "The Lord looks down from heaven and sees the whole human race. From his throne, he observes all who live on the earth. He made their hearts, so he understands everything they do." God understands our skewed mentalities, our lust, and our struggles, and instead of turning away, He offers to love us through it all. He works with us, empowering us to overcome those things that would keep us in rebelling.

Walking in Pride

I never really thought about the power of humility in resisting the pull toward disobedience. When it came to temptation and honoring God, I understood that humility was generally necessary. Still, I hadn't comprehended the stability and strength it gave to a believer who was confronting temptation. In the battle of resisting unrighteousness, my first defense was usually self-control. However, James 4:7 instructs us first to maintain a humble mindset in the face of temptation, then utilize restraint to resist the temptation. How we see ourselves affects how we handle the attraction to wickedness, and the enemy knows it. The serpent's interaction with Eve showed us a pattern of communication with the enemy that leads to rebellion. The serpent questions Eve about how the foundation of her faith entices her and then discredits the warnings of God all within a few moments of talking. The enemy's tactic to attract and flatter works because we are more prone to sin when we think more of ourselves than we should. He tells us we deserve more and then instructs us on how to get it using his means, sin. God warns against pride because it takes our eyes off Him and places them on the self. Pride is a gateway that leads us away from righteousness and into sin.

Our hearts are no different from those of our predecessors. Just as Adam and Eve allowed unrighteous pride to tarnish the blessing of communion with God, so do we today. Humanity views God differently. Some people choose to ignore His loving grace, some take delight in a relationship with God, some despise Him, some deny His existence, and some replace Him with false idols. It is in pride that we choose not to acknowledge and honor Him. Proverbs 16:18 says that "pride goes before destruction and haughtiness before a fall." When we separate ourselves from God, we separate ourselves from the source of life, and it places us in a weak position, spiritually, mentally, and emotionally. Unrighteous pride is harmful because it causes us to overstep boundaries set up to protect us, and it doesn't consider what is right, only one's desires. It stems from the misconceptions that we deserve that which we have not earned and that we can take what is not rightfully ours.

In Genesis 3, the conversation between the serpent and Eve in the garden of Eden signals the entrance of pride. The serpent's words tempt Eve and Adam to disobey God with the idea that they deserve more. The serpent discredits God's love in its conversation with Eve. Then it encourages Adam and Eve to disregard their connection with God and question His motives. Because of pride, they seek more power and ultimately walk in disobedience in an attempt to be God. Blinded by their ego, they question God's integrity. Without realizing it, they try to get something through defiance that God has freely given them through their relationship with Him. They seek to become God by rebelling when God has already made them in His image, giving them authority over everything on earth. Pride drastically changed the nature of humanity from something God called good to something plagued with sin. Pride disfigures character, relationships, and vision. In *The Dake Study Bible*, minister and evangelist Finis Dake describes the opening of Adam and Eve's eyes as a forfeiture of God's consciousness and the acquisition of self-consciousness. Their nature changed from one that sought goodness to one that found evil. Ironically, in their pursuit to become more like God, they became less like Him.

Adam and Eve had no grounds for disobedience then, and we have none today. Everything that the world offers through unrighteous acts and rebellion, God offers to us freely through relationship. Yet when temptation speaks to our ego, we often listen, disregarding the love of God and subsequently walking in disobedience. When Satan tempts Jesus in Matthew 4, he offers Jesus worldly power and influence if Jesus would ignore God and instead worship him. Jesus, knowing the Word of the Father, did not entertain the thought of questioning God's integrity or disregarding His communion with the Father. We should respond to temptation with confidence in the words of God's promise and His love for us, committed to our purpose of a relationship with Him.

We can find temptation all around us and should not be anxious or fearful of this fact because, in truth, temptation comes from within (James 1:14). The only way to overcome that part of us that wants to do wrong is choosing to do right. The lure of sinful acts should not make us timid about living and experiencing life and its abundance, but it should call us to be watchful, prayerful, and grounded in God. We need only to avoid deviating from the path of righteousness, and we are kept safe from the grip of sin. Some would say, "Easier said than done," and that is true. However, Jesus never said that walking a righteous path would be easy. He told us that living a life that honored in a world that despised Him would be hard, but it is not impossible. It is easier, however, when we use the tools that Jesus has given us and our companion, the Holy Spirit. God did not remove the temptation for Adam, Eve, or Jesus, and He will not remove the temptation for us. But God does give us a way to escape. He provides us with the power and authority of His Word to stand on and free will to reject the temptation, as Christ demonstrated in Matthew 4:1–11. God is always there for us, waiting to minister to us in our time of need. We just have to look to Him and be wise enough to reject what the devil is offering. God's Word holds power, and that works in the time of temptation. When faced with temptation, we should not waiver on the meaning of God's Word, as Eve did. Adam and Eve knew the words that God spoke, but when confronted, they must not have understood its power, because they discarded the words of God for the ideas of a serpent.

Penalty of Sin

The consequence of their sin was a sinful nature that brought about death physically and spiritually. This sinful nature made accomplishing Adam and Eve's purpose harder, but it did not change it. God still wanted them to populate the earth and subdue it in a matter that honored Him. The curses God placed on each of the offenders were a form of punishment, but it did not undo the consequences of the wrong they had committed. Their actions had irreversible repercussions, so God banished them from the garden of Eden to prevent them from eating of the tree of life. God disciplines to encourage the correction of ungodly behaviors and mentalities. If He allowed Adam, Eve, and the serpent to go unpunished, there would have been nothing tangible to encourage and remind them to rethink rebellion in the future. They would have gone away from that transgression believing that God was not a God of His Word, that He condoned disobedience and that dishonoring Him had no consequences. David explained his process of learning to follow God's Word in Psalm 119:67–68: "I used to wander off until you disciplined me, but now I closely follow your word. You are good and do only good; teach me your decrees." The priest Eli's sons exemplify the results of condoning bad behavior and sin without correction: it just gets worse. In 2 Samuel 2, Eli's wicked sons stole the sacrificial offerings reserved for God, but they also sinned against the people and seduced the women serving in the tabernacle. Eli knew all this, and instead of removing them from their position and disciplining them for their deeds, he allowed them to continue serving in a place of honor and power, disserving God and His people. Eli, the head of the house, did not hold them accountable for their immoral behavior and open dishonor toward God. His sons showed no signs of remorse or turning back from the desecration of God's offering and temple. How long had Eli tolerated his sons' disobedience for them to have such a disregard for God? God handled the problem that Eli was unwilling to correct, and He punished them by removing Eli's lineage from serving in the priesthood and taking their lives. In 1 Samuel 2:30, God declares, "I will honor those who honor me, and I will despise those who think lightly of me."

God has established boundaries and rules to protect humanity from the chaos and destruction of sin. Consequences of disobedience keep us from wandering toward destruction. Every believer should see the importance of correction and receive it, realizing its purpose to guide us back to the right path. "I correct and discipline everyone I love. So be diligent and turn from your indifference" (Rev. 3:19). The principles and dictates of God are for us to honor and uphold. Our actions and decisions have consequences that can spread beyond ourselves. Some people do not care about the repercussions it has to others, so penalties and discipline are needed to constrain their readiness to do whatever they please.

As Christians, we do not need to worry about being judged for our sins (John 5:24) because of Christ. However, we are still subject to discipline and consequences, which discourage wickedness and encourage us to be more like Christ. He disciplines to turn us from our sinful behavior and helps us to handle life more righteously. "For he disciplines those he loves, and he punishes each one he accepts as his child" (Heb. 12:6). Some people may argue that God would not sentence anyone to an eternity of suffering because He is a loving God. When we search the Word of God, we see that He is not only love and gives grace but He is also a God of justice and discipline and has instituted the principals of reaping and sowing. God did not change Adam's and Eve's consequences for eating from the tree; he showed them mercy by providing a way for redemption and provided for them and the generation to follow a Savior. Through the sacrifice of Jesus Christ, God's Son, for the redemption of our souls. Those who receive this grace through faith in Jesus Christ are rescued from experiencing the ultimate cost and consequence of sin. We circumvent our path to damnation by accepting Jesus's work on the cross.

God's Provision

When Adam and Eve sinned, the justice God established before their creation required life as payment for their transgression (Rom. 6:23). God created a system of sacrificial offerings to atone for humanity's sin and pay its debt. God had mercy on Adam and Eve. He sacrificed an animal to cover the outward manifestation of their sin with animal skin, and the animal's lifeblood stood in for the blood that Christ would shed for us all on Calvary. Hebrew 9:22 informs us that "without the shedding of blood, there is no remission" of sin. Only sacrificial offerings are acceptable to cover the debt of sin. Leviticus 4:22 tells us sacrificial offerings provide atonement for sins so that forgiveness can be issued.

In Genesis 4, we see that Adam and Eve taught their children, Cain and Abel, this principle, and they brought animal sacrifices to God. Yet Cain was reluctant to follow the dictates of God. Instead, he offered vegetation. Abel followed what was mandated; he acknowledged his sinfulness and need for God's mercy by offering an animal sacrifice. God corrected Cain in verses 6–7: "'Why are you so angry?' the LORD asked Cain. 'Why do you look so dejected? You will be accepted if you do what is right. But if you refuse to do what is right, then watch out! Sin is crouching at the door, eager to control you. But you must subdue it and be its master.'" We can see God's grace and patience with humanity. He gives Cain grace and allows him the opportunity to correct himself, yet Cain chooses rebellion and murders his brother. Humanity can refuse God's love and grace and decide to stay in sin and reap its consequences.

These animal sacrifices were a temporary substitution for the everlasting act that Christ would perform. Jesus was always the plan of salvation even before the earth's creation. However, Christ's appointed time was not until thousands of years after Adam and Eves' transgression. Between the fall and Jesus's crucifixion, God allows humanity to sacrifice animals to show their repentance and need for a Savior. God loved us so much that He offered His own Son as a sacrifice to reconcile us to Him. Jesus came to the earth as a man so that He could experience what we experience in temptation and suffering. Jesus took the position as our high priest and pleaded for mercy on our behalf before God. Then He sacrificed His life so that the debt of our sins could be washed away with His blood.

Adam's act of disobedience brought about the inherent sin sickness of humanity. It was as if he introduced a spiritual genetic mutation to what God once called good. The only way to cure this illness and pay for our sins so that we would not have to experience damnation was a holy sacrifice, and only Jesus could afford to pay the cost and heal our soul. Jesus's obedience to the Father led Him to offer healing and deliverance from sin and death. Romans 5:18–19 tells us this:

> Yes, Adam's one sin brings condemnation for everyone, but Christ's one act of righteousness brings a right relationship with God and new life for everyone. Because one person disobeyed God, many became sinners. But because one other person obeyed God, many will be made righteous.

God's original plan did not include death for humanity but everlasting life. Since the fall, death signifies the end of humanity's journey on this earth. Death is a consequence of the fall, but damnation does not have to be the end. God's love provided means of redemption so that all who believed in Jesus's redemptive work could receive salvation from damnation on the day of judgment. As Hebrews 9:27 tells us, "each person is destined to die once and after that comes judgment." Those who choose to stay under Satan's influence will reap the same reward as him. God gives His love and grace, and anyone who refuses them will not be exempt from the penalty of disobedience: eternal damnation. Those who have accepted the grace and love that God offers receive salvation and become a part of the kingdom of God.

Summary

We must work to stop the cycle of sin in our lives that Adam and Eve introduced by walking away from their purpose and the following pride. We make daily choices to either honor God or please the flesh. Let's commit ourselves to yield to the transformation of salvation and overcoming those things that try to hinder us from honoring God. As believers, we no longer have to worry about damnation; we have been redeemed and empowered to become like Christ because God provides mercy and grace. God will discipline those who stray to show them the wisdom of staying on the path, which is paved with His blessings and leads us to abundant life. We must guard ourselves against pride by learning and heeding the Word of God, staying humble, and yielding to God's wisdom. We must allow for His perfect timing so we may receive our blessings and promises. There are entities at play that will try to hinder and oppress us. We must be wise to their devices and seek God for guidance and strength in our efforts to live righteously and honor Him.

PERPETUATING *the* STRUGGLE

The Fall of Creation: The Prequel

Humanity was not the first of God's creations to rebel. Satan, a once-high-ranking angel in heaven, allowed his ambition for more power and glory to drive him to revolt against God and encouraged a third of the angels to do the same. God's army defeated Satan and the other rebellious angels, and they had been judged and thrust out of heaven. Jesus says in Luke 10:18, "'Yes,' he told them, 'I saw Satan fall from heaven like lightning!'" The storyline of the fall of Satan and the other angels bleeds into humanity's narrative and colors it. The enemies' hatred and rebellion toward God did not end with their defeat and judgment; they continue to rebel against God by manipulating humanity as pawns, leading, deceiving, and encouraging them to rebel and reject an intimate relationship with the Creator. After their eyes of understanding opened in the garden of Eden, Satan and his camp perpetuated and encouraged sin in God's beloved creation. The fall gave the enemy a way to undermine the purpose of the kingdom of God on this earth. Satan entices humanity to rebel against God to make a mockery of His beloved creation. He and his camp of demons and principalities will continue to further his agenda until the appointed time of their already-determined end.

The Enemy's Soldiers

We wrestle against not only Satan but also his camp, "evil rulers and authorities of the unseen world, against mighty powers in this dark world, and against evil spirits in the heavenly places" (Eph. 6:12). We struggle with entities called demons or evil spirits, which are unable to operate in the physical world unless they inhabit man or beast. In Mark 5:9–13, Jesus encountered a man possessed by a horde of demons, Legion, and instead of condemning them to hell, He allowed them to continue their works of mischief. Mark 5:13 tells us that Jesus permitted them to continue their activity on this earth, and they entered into a herd of pigs. Why are demons allowed to roam the land if they are such menaces, and why is Satan allowed to exist when he causes such chaos? A parable Jesus shared in Matthew 13:24–30 speaks to the formation of the kingdom of heaven. In the parable, the farmer allows the wheat and the weeds to grow together. At harvest, he separates the two by tossing the weeds in the fire and gathering the wheat into the barns. Similarly, God allows all His creation to coinhabit this universe; in His wisdom He will separate them at the appointed time.

We must understand and believe that God is Almighty, and we must live in peace knowing that God allows the good and bad to coinhabit this universe. We may fear and dislike the presence of an enemy, but the enemy's end is determined. Satan is defeated in our lives through Christ's work on the cross. Satan continues to rebel against God, but his activities are monitored and restrained by God, and he is allowed to operate because he ultimately brings about the will of God. As believers, we must find peace knowing "that God causes everything to work together for the good of those who love God and are called according to His purpose for them" (Rom. 8:28).

Satan, the other principalities, and demons will receive their final punishment at their appointed time, just as humans. They can operate within the constraints that God dictates. Pending the start of their sentence, these demons will continue to work with Satan and pursue his agenda to kill, steal, and destroy humanity. The enemy moves on every front, trying to influence our spiritual, mental, emotional, and physical state. They work to keep the lost bound and the saved oppressed, by engaging one or many aspects of our being. The enemies of our souls create and encourage unhealthy, unproductive states within us to impede us from fulfilling our purpose effectively. In *The Screwtape Letters*, C. S. Lewis creates a fictional one-sided conversation between a demon named Screwtape and his protégé nephew Wormwood. In the letters, Screwtape shares techniques and strategies that guide his nephew in hindering the spiritual, emotional, and mental state of a newly converted believer so that he does not walk in the abundant life Christ has provided and draw closer in relationship with God. The accounts are fictional; however, they illustrate just how diligently, relentlessly, and deceptively the enemy works to keep the believers from growing and the lost soul from receiving salvation.

Demons have different modes by which they influence and manipulate humanity, including possession. The evil spirit's nature is to try to possess the living. For example, Matthew 12:43–44 says, "When an evil spirit leaves a person, it goes into the desert, seeking rest but finding none. Then it says, 'I will return to the person I came from.' So it returns and finds its former home empty, swept, and in order." The Old Testament scripture reveals that devil worship is not new and demons not only played unseen roles by possessing living creatures but also persuaded humanity to think of them as gods. Deuteronomy 32:17 tells us that people "offered sacrifices to demons, which are not God, to gods they had not known before, to new gods only recently arrived, to gods their ancestors had never feared." The enemy does not only distract humanity from honoring and loving God but also provide substitutions for God with the hope that humanity will not see a need for God.

Satan and demons have power and influence, but they are all limited and regulated by God. Legion, the horde of demons in the verses of Mark 5, understood who Jesus was and knew His authority and power. That was why one of them asked Jesus for leniency and permission. The believer should not cower or fear in the face of demons and their suggestions or attacks. James tells us to resist the evil one and he will be the one to run away:

But you belong to God, my dear children. You have already won a victory over those people because the

Spirit who lives in you is greater than the spirit who lives in the world. The Spirit of God lives within the believer, so Satan has no power over them unless we relinquish that power of influence to him. (1 John 4:4)

Believers Are Free from Satan's Control

Satan had dominion over us when we were in darkness, but no longer. We are no longer under his sphere of control now that we have received deliverance and walk in the light. Hearing the good news of Christ opens our eyes. It steers us away from the dark powers of Satan toward a life-transforming relationship with God that offers deliverance and forgiveness (Acts 26:17b–18). Receiving the good news of salvation makes us a part of God's kingdom and gives us the Spirit of God. In this renewed state, Satan no longer has control over the believer and cannot make them do anything. Satan and demons can entice and influence the believer, but they do not have authority over the believer. When Jesus talked to God about the well-being of His disciples, He spoke not of rescuing us from the temptation and hardships of this world; he spoke of keeping us safe from the evil one (John 17:15). We will have to encounter and war against the influencing of this world, but we do not have to worry about them overtaking our saved souls, because God has vowed to keep us safe.

Because of the authority that Jesus has given us through His name and the Spirit of God that seal us, we have the power to cast out demons (Luke 10:19, Mark 16:17). When we come against a devil in the authority of Jesus's name, they have to listen. When we understand this, it helps to overcome the paranoia and fearfulness of the enemy. We gain confidence in our ability to defeat demons and overcome Satan's sphere of influence because of our stance in Christ.

We have power, but there remain many who have yet to accept God's gift of salvation and remain under Satan's control. Paul writes, "Satan, who is the god of this world, has blinded the minds of those who don't believe. They are unable to see the glorious light of the Good News. They don't understand this message about the glory of Christ, who is the exact likeness of God" (2 Cor. 4:4). Satan is deceptive and has fooled many into believing that they do not need God or can settle for any version of a god. Those who choose to follow Satan can be just as deceptive and persuade others to reject the good news and its life-changing, destination-rearranging power and purpose.

Oppression and Possession

Paul saw the need to remind the church in Ephesus about the nature of our real enemy. He states, "For we are not fighting against flesh-and-blood enemies, but against evil rulers and authorities of the unseen world, against mighty powers in this dark world, and against evil spirits in the heavenly places" (Eph. 6:12). We fight against an enemy today who wants to destroy humanity and come against our purpose. They want to usurp God's designated position in our lives. The enemy knows the love God has for His creation and therefore focuses their efforts to destroy us. They can influence humanity and the things of this earth because Adam and Eve relinquished their dominion over it when they sinned against God. They can affect us through possession and oppression. Possession is when a demon inhabits one and is controlled by that demon. But believers cannot be possessed, because the Spirit of God lives in us. So, the enemy wars against us with oppression instead, influencing situations and introducing thoughts. We must identify these thoughts and cast them out. We must recognize these situations and retain a godly character so that we bring glory to God, even in the enemy's attempts at oppression.

Act 16:16–26 is an example of how the enemy uses possession and oppression against the believer to hinder the works of God. Paul was preaching the gospel in Europe with Silas. On this particular day, they were heading to prayer when they encountered a slave girl possessed by a spirit that could tell the future. As they passed her, she proclaimed that Paul and Silas were servants of God who would show everyone the way to salvation. The demon had the girl speak the truth, but he wanted the people of the town to link Paul and Silas with the fortune-teller so that he could attribute their work to that of the demons. Paul recognized the motive of the evil spirit and cast him out of the girl. Her master became upset when he realized what happened, because he knew that he could no longer profit from the girl's fortune-telling. He brought allegations against Paul and Silas, and they were bound in stocks, beaten, and thrown into prison. Instead of being discouraged, Paul and Silas prayed and sang of praises to God. The other prisoners heard them, and when God caused an earthquake that opened the doors and shackles of the prison, the jailer realized that the miracle was from Paul and Silas's God. He also understood the trouble he would be in if the prisoners escaped, but Paul and Silas did not run away. When the jailer saw that they didn't try to escape, he asked them how he to receive salvation. Paul and Silas did not allow people or situations to dictate who they were; they knew their calling and held fast to their faith and integrity. They stood steady in their spiritual liberty and honored God and maintained a demeanor of authority and kept their peace in God.

Some may view Paul's and Silas's imprisonment as a victory for the enemy, but it was a second attempt at oppressing Paul and Silas. Christ said that we would have to suffer persecution for his namesake, and Paul and Silas chose to endure the suffering admirably. They were even able to lead the jailer into a relationship with Christ because they maintained godly character. In the face of slander, violence, and imprisonment, they let the light of Christ shine. Paul and Silas stood firm in Christ and gained the victory. Paul was a Roman citizen, and they were released because of it. Even when it looks like the enemy is winning, God has a plan. When we follow God's guidance and maintain the character of God, the enemy always loses. The circumstance may not change how we want them, yet God can get the glory out of them. The enemy loses ground when we, as believers, resist ungodly actions. Our real opponents and enemies are not flesh-and-blood people but the invisible entities that influence them, and we can educate ourselves so that we are not ignorant of their devices and actions. God gives us what we need to resist and fight against them effectively.

The influence of the enemy in the believer's or unbeliever's life can be subtle or blatant. When Paul encountered the slave girl with her pronouncements, it was an ingenious way for the enemy to try to associate God with the works of a fortune-teller. Paul recognized the real enemy and spoke to the demon who had possessed her and told him to come out. Many people are unaware of the enemy's hold on their lives. The enemy feeds their emotions, their desires, and their fears while devising a plan to oppress the people of God and keep the lost soul blind and bound in sin. The enemy plays a long game. He studies the behavior of humanity and deciphers our fears and desires. The enemy utilizes this information cunningly so that we do not readily discern his movement or motives, but with the insight of the Holy Spirit, we can see things for what they are. Some people are aware of their role in the enemy's plan and are proud of their involvement. Others are in the dark. Jesus said of the people who chanted His demise, "Father, forgive them for they do not know what they are doing" (Luke 23:34). They persecuted Christ in ignorance, but the consequence of their sin remained until Jesus chose to show mercy. Ignorance does not excuse one from the effects of sin and submitting to the enemy, but it is forgivable, and people can be redeemed. Hosea 4:6a reads, "My people are destroyed for lack of knowledge: because thou hast rejected knowledge, I will also reject thee." As the Body of Christ, we combat against this destructive ignorance by sharing the Word of God, praying that others will see and receive the truth.

The Response of the Believer

God calls us to a higher standard of interaction with the world. He knows the influence that the demons and principalities can have, but He also knows the more significant impact that believers can have if they abide in Him. Jesus tells us, in Matthew 5:44–48, to love, bless, do good, and pray for those who treat us poorly. He said this because Christians no longer live by the same standards of a society that seeks an eye for an eye and tooth for a tooth. We are to be beacons of light for a dark world. How can we do that if we play the same games of revenge and hate? You never know how your actions influence those around you. We have a right to our emotions, thoughts, and even feelings of anger. However, these emotions and opinions do not grant us a license to sin.

The spiritual world and the physical world are so intertwined that we sometimes misidentify the actual problems and solutions. Most of our spiritual weapons and gifts manifest themselves through tangible means, like love. Love is patient, kind, and forgiving. These things are intangible, but they manifest themselves in discernable ways—speech and action. As Christians, we must allow ourselves to mature and accept what God gives and says to us so that the spiritual gifts God has freely given may manifest themselves tangibly in our lives. When we take this initiative, we can effectively fight against the oppression of the enemy. However, if we choose other means to resist the enemy, we set ourselves up for failure because earthly and fleshly tactics do not work against a spiritual enemy. We spend so much time interacting with the physical world that we mistakenly try to tackle spiritually oriented problems through natural means. We are to consult God in everything. Proverbs 3:5–6 advises us, "Trust in the LORD with all your heart; do not depend on your own understanding. Seek His will in all you do, and He will show you which path to take." When we call on God, He may divinely intervene or guide us in utilizing the tools that He provides us, such as patience, love, forgiving, and repentance. The various tools God offers should always be among our answers to confronting the issues of our lives. We can always seek further wisdom from God through His Word, prayer, and other grounded believers when we are unable to figure out how to apply those tools tangibly.

Satan is relentless in his quest to disprove and condemn humanity, especially redeemed believers. He will continuously come against us, but we must know that God does not allow those tests to destroy us but to show Satan, ourselves, and the world what the redemptive work of Christ and the presence of His Spirit can do for humanity. God's Spirit sustains the believer during our struggles and even in failure. Some of us have not reached Job's level of spiritual maturity to say, "Naked I came, naked I will go," and mean it. However, as we continue to depend on and grow in God, we become more competent in our walk and overcome Satan's daily attempt to oppress us.

Jesus's Redeeming Influence

Once you were dead because of your disobedience and your many sins. You used to live in sin, just like the rest of the world, obeying the devil, the commander of the powers in the unseen world. He is the spirit at work in the hearts of those who refuse to obey God. All of us used to live that way, following the passionate desires and inclinations of our sinful nature. By our very nature we were subject to God's anger, just like everyone else. But God is so rich in mercy and He loved us so much that even though we were dead because of our sins, he gave us life when he raised Christ from the dead. (It is only by God's grace that you have been saved [Eph.2:1–5]).

When Adam sinned, he let down the standard, and Satan's presence and influence entered this world like a flood, corrupting the purpose that God gave it. Jesus, the Redeemer, stopped the reign of Satan over the believer. Jesus, our Redeemer, has taken us back and purified us. When Christ died on the cross and rose again, He came back planting His standard, His flag, letting Satan know that He has come to claim what is His. Satan has no authority or control over those who are God's. Peter tells us in Peter 5:8, "Stay alert! Watch out for your great enemy, the devil. He prowls around like a roaring lion, looking for someone to devour."

When one chooses to receive Christ's redemptive work, it does not pause the enemy's plan. This choice transplants us from one side of the battlefield to the other. We be vigilant (1 Pet. 3:5), continue in prayer (1 Thess. 5:17), and yield to the will of God (James 4:7) so that we can be useful in our walk with

Christ. Our failures and missteps do not change whose side we are on, because once we accept Christ as our Savior, we are His. However, if we are slow to mature and establish healthy natural and spiritual habits, we will see more defeats than victories. Neglecting good habits will hinder us from experiencing the fullness of the abundant life Christ provides. Satan uses the sinner as well as the saint to accomplish his purpose. Before being saved, we were exploited by the enemy, often ignorantly, but now we are no longer ignorant of his devices. We act sometimes based on lust, other times on emotions, and even in logic. The enemy draws us into doing his bidding, but we are still held accountable for our choices in the end.

In Matthew 16:16–17, Peter proclaims that Jesus is "the Christ, the son of the Living God." Peter was sensitive to the things of God and received revelation from heaven about who Jesus was. However, soon after, in verse 23, Jesus was rebuking Peter and called him Satan. How did Peter so quickly change from a tool of heavenly revelation to being used by Satan? The verses between these events detail Jesus's conversation with the disciples about His looming persecution, death, and resurrection. Peter felt the need to object to the horrible things that Christ had to go through because of his relationship with Christ. Peter thought he could change the will of God. When Peter rebuked Jesus, he contradicted Jesus's very purpose on this earth—to become a sacrifice and the Savior of the world.

Peter allowed the enemy to use his emotions and opinions to lure Him into walking in sin. Peter thought he spoke the words as a show of loyalty and support, but they were words of discouragement and opposition. Jesus saw these words for what they indeed were—an offense and an attack against His purpose and God's will. He saw the work of the enemy in Peter's words, and He rebuked him. The Word of God informs us how cunning and ruthless the enemy is. God's Word advises us to be vigilant, watchful, and cautious (1 Pet. 5:8). The enemy utilizes whatever he can to oppose God and oppress humanity. Our emotions and opinions are some of those lures he uses, and we must be aware of these things, allowing God's Word to guide us. We should not build our response to emotions and opinions.

Summary

Sin, which is disobedience, and rebellion, is the source of sickness within our souls, and our desire for it causes us to struggle. Satan, the enemy of our soul, did not make sin, but he does entice us to participate in it because of its corrupt nature that dishonors our relationship with God. Through Christ's sacrifice, we have been made right in God's sight, and the debt of sin no longer separates us from a relationship with God. Sin, however, is still used as a tool to keep the Body of Christ sick, hindered, and not walking in the fullness of God's promises. The enemy wants to oppress the believer. In this fallen world, we will have to endure the effects of evil and the draw of sin, but we should not cower in the face of it. Christ has equipped and graced us to deal righteously with the variety of wickedness found in this world. The world will tempt us to embrace its immorality and sell us on its fleeting pleasures. There will be frequent opposition to our walk of righteousness, and we must remember the power inside of us given through God's Spirit, which enables us to overcome during these moments. This strength is not something we manufacture, but it comes from God. We are empowered through His Spirit so that we can resist temptation and overcome the enemy in a way that honors and glorifies Him.

Satan is an opposer of the Body of Christ, and he will use whatever tools he can to keep humanity from having a relationship with Christ or oppressing those who do have a relationship with Him. We, as the Body of Christ, must be sure of our purpose and diligent in our efforts to care for one another if we are to put up a strong front. When we falter in our mission of loving God with all our heart, soul, strength, and mind and following that up with loving our neighbors as ourselves (Luke 10:27), we give the enemy opportunity to operate. We must become aware of the tricks of the enemy and resist His attempts to usurp control in our lives.

PART 2

Purpose and Care

GOD'S AGENDA
of LOVE

In a public health course in undergrad, I began to identify spiritual truths during some of the history lessons. I was sitting in a lecture about the historical use of antiseptics and its drastic impact on decreasing hospital mortality rates and the spread of disease. The majority of us use antiseptics today, and most of us carry some form of disinfectant with us to combat common everyday germs. However, people did not accept the need for antiseptics in the medical field, in which they deal daily with the sickly and susceptible, until the late 1800s. In 1840, Dr. Ignaz Semmelweis, an Austrian obstetrician, grew concerned with the high rate of childbed fever, an infection that can occur after childbirth and often ends in death. He noticed that five times fewer incidents happened in the ward attended by midwives, as opposed to physicians and medical students. Dr. Semmelweis investigated to identify the cause. After witnessing a fellow physician die from sickness after working on a corpse, he suspected that an open cut allowed the physician to become sick. They did not know about pathogens, bacteria, and viruses at this time, but Semmelweis did conclude that the corpses and the physicians who worked on them shared something harmful. Midwives did not work with bodies, and he found that physicians passed on something from the bodies that caused childbed fever in birthing women. He came up with the germ theory and encouraged the practice of washing hands and medical instruments with soap and chlorine after working with corpses in his institution.

He saw a drastic decrease in childbed fever after implementing these practices and shared his findings with the medical community, but many turned a deaf ear. His conclusions did not align with the teachings of his time. Dr. Semmelweis was ostracized rather than commended by his fellow physicians. They ignored the importance of his findings, leaving patients to suffer unnecessarily and often die because the professionals simply refused to receive wisdom and prevent infection by washing their hands. Their unwillingness to see the merit of handwashing led to many preventable deaths. The medical community did not recognize the use of antiseptics until decades later, when Dr. Joseph Lister, who concluded the same thing, published a successful surgery under sterile conditions.

This story resembles what Paul discusses in the book of Romans. In chapters 14 and 15, Paul acknowledges the presence of weaker or less mature saints and admonishes the stronger, more mature saints to handle them as such. He says, "We who are strong must be considerate of those who are sensitive about things like this. We must not just please ourselves. We should help others do what is right and build them up in the Lord" (Rom.

15:1–2). Those physicians who were, for the most part, healthy individuals were not affected by the germs from the corpses because they did not have any wounds or openings that the bacteria could enter. They felt at liberty to ignore cleanliness. The women giving birth and the individuals undergoing surgery had vulnerable incisions and sores that the germs could infect and make them sick. However, these physicians didn't recognize their role or responsibility for spreading these germs because they didn't have these vulnerabilities and did not suffer the same afflictions. Those physicians did not want to take the extra necessary steps, even when they were simple, to prevent the additional hurt of those in their care. Rather than acknowledge the danger and avoid spread by simply washing their hands, they allowed many more to die and continued to blame other things for their patients' deaths. The same happens in the Body of Christ today. Some saints are so busy walking in their liberty that they do not see the adverse effects their behavior and mentality have on the less mature saints and unbelievers. The stronger believer should come alongside the weaker, encouraging them, building them up in wisdom so that they grow stronger.

We must take care of the Body of Christ to avoid causing others to "stumble and fall" (Rom. 14:13–15). History and these verses shine a light on the negative impact of ignorance and how we can cause undue harm by not acknowledging our responsibility to one another. Satan is not the only force that harms the Body of Christ. Sometimes the believer's ignorance, laziness, and pride can be just as harmful and hinder the purpose of God. The members of the Body of Christ can be their own worst enemy when they are careless or unknowledgeable. Believers should maintain and build up the Body of Christ through wisdom and compassion. God gives the believer many tools and principles to effectively support one another and promote healing, growth, and development. Each believer must consider the other members; life is about not only individual comfort and triumph but also the building up and loving of others. We are reminded in John 13:34, "Love each other. Just as I have loved you, you should love each other."

The Purpose of the Body of Christ

God has a universal, divine purpose for the Body of Christ. It is to reveal and testify of His manifold wisdom to the universe's "unseen rulers and authorities in heavenly places" (Eph. 3:8–19). The Body of Christ is a testament to God's grace, mercy, and power amid rebellion and wickedness. We display the wisdom and love of God's plan for salvation through Christ for humanity. The Body shows the universe that those with free will can faithfully honor and serve God in the face of opposition through His empowerment: "And having chosen them, he called them to come to him. And having called them, he gave them right standing with himself. And having given them right standing, he gave them his glory" (Rom. 8:30). Through God's wisdom and love, the body is being delivered and cleansed of rebellion.

It is a privileged and a blessing to be part of the Body of Christ. We should not allow the distraction and frustration of life to preoccupy our minds and cause us to forget the authority, power, and guidance that come with that position. The believer should walk worthy of the good news and reciprocate the dedicated and faithful love that God has shown us. This dedication and faithfulness should be evident in our everyday practices and our relationship with God. Each member of the Body is grafted into the kingdom of God for a purpose. The believer must acknowledge their part and prayerfully do it with excellence. Each member is in a different stage of development and knowledge, but all are on the path to becoming more like Christ. Each part must encourage one another during the process and recruit more into the Body.

We promote healing and growth in others by contributing and acting as a productive part of the Body of Christ. God does not want the Body sick. We receive those who are suffering into the Body so that they can receive healing. Healing is a process, and untying oneself from habits, addictions, faults, mannerisms, and skewed thinking takes patience and love. When one becomes a part of the body, they yield themselves to the process of healing and development. They avail themselves to encourage and support others on their journey of healing. Just as God is patient and loving toward humanity, the believer must be the same. "Most important of all," believers must "continue to show deep love for each other, for love covers a multitude of sins" (1 Pet. 4:8). God uses the tool of love to bring about a change in the heart that receives His Son. He doesn't use anger, judgment, or condemnation, so the believer should not use them either. Paul describes how the body should interact in Ephesians 4:15–16: "We will speak the truth in love, growing in every way more and more like Christ, who is the head of his body, the church. He makes the whole body fit together perfectly. As each part does its special work, it helps the other parts grow, so that the whole body is healthy and growing and full of love." When we work in harmony and deal with one another in love, we become more like Christ.

We should not allow disagreements and differences of opinions to cause division among the Body. We should look to God with understanding, compassion, and patience to resolve the issues that arise. The Body has been called together for a purpose, and it is counterintuitive to let disagreements come in and hinder that purpose. A difference of opinion should not impede the sharing of the gospel of God's love. "Let all who are spiritually mature agree on these things. If you disagree on some point, I believe God will make it plain to you. But we must hold on to the progress we have already made" (Phil. 3:15–16). We should not uphold or validate contradictions to the Word of God, but neither should we cease to show the love of God. Believers who hold on to old opinions and ideas without first consulting God's Word can create confusion in the community of faith and lead others astray. Worldly opinions and ideas can cause us to stunt our growth or create a stumbling block for others.

We should put away our brand of wisdom after salvation, and we should seek God's wisdom. As it says in Psalm 51:10, "Create in me a clean heart, O God. Renew a loyal spirit within me." God cleanses and renews us through His Spirit, and Christ brings peace to the body. Walking in this renewed state is the believer's job. We can still choose to forgo this state and resume our old ways of thinking and doing, after receiving all this from God. So the believer should stay alert and diligent to prevent their past life from casting darkness on their relationships and renewed purpose. If we let this state go, our past may lead us to discord (Amos 3:3), which opposes the unification that Christ is creating. When we accept our role in the Body of Christ, we declare that we are willing to unify with whomever else God receives unto His body.

Unity and Peace

We must remember that our differences do not make us enemies, and they also do not make us lesser or more significant in the eyes of God. We are all His beloved creation. Whoever Christ has called blessed, no one can try to disqualify them from His mercies. Ephesians 2:16–18 instructs us to put our hostility toward others to death. God has chosen to reconcile to whoever receives the works of Christ by His Spirit.

Prejudice. In the book of Galatians, Paul confronts Peter about his hypocrisy and his prejudiced acts in Galatians 2:11–13. Peter followed peace and unity with non-Jewish believers until a few fellow Jews showed up. He went along with bigoted rhetoric, discarding the revelation God had given Him. The kingdom of God is for all who will receive the works of Christ on the cross. Their actions and words ran contrary to God's mandate of love and grace, but to stay on good terms with them, Peter did not confront them. He did not correct them in their extreme attitudes or acknowledge his disagreement with it. Paul confronted Peter in public because Peter's prejudiced actions influenced others and encouraged hypocrisy. Paul brought Peter's attention to the fact that he was reverting to old ways, which did not bring honor to God. When a believer joins a crowd whose ideals run contrary to God, they become hypocrites. God does not want hypocrites, only believers who see that their old way of thinking and biased group affirmation brings no benefit to walking in the righteous path with integrity and unity.

Hate. The way we love the world will let others know that we belong to God. God is a God of love, and people's list for hate does not detour God's message of love. He does not condone hate even when it feels justifiable. Jonah, an Old Testament prophet of God, walked in hatred toward Nineveh, an enemy of the Israelites. They had a history of persecuting God's people, and Jonah refused to minister to them. Jonah chose hate and wanted the destruction of Nineveh. He refused to preach the message of judgment because he knew that God was merciful and would save the people of Nineveh if they repented. Once Jonah finally yielded to God's will, Nineveh not only heard but also heeded the message Jonah delivered. They repented, and God showed them the mercy that Jonah did not want them to receive. Jonah was beholden more to his hate than to God's desire to transform and change thousands of lives. Hatred and our reluctance to accept others do not change God's love and compassion toward humanity. Our stubbornness to hold on to darkness and choose hate over love only causes us to want revenge over God. John 4:20 informs us that "if someone says, 'I love God,' but hates a fellow believer, that person is a liar; for if we don't love people we can see, how can we love God, whom we cannot see?"

We are to live in humility and be patient as we work together to achieve the same goals. To do this, we must maintain righteous attitudes so that hard times and difficult people will not cause us to lose focus on our endeavors to serve and honor God. We are to "always be humble and gentle. Be patient with each other, making allowance for each other's faults because of your love. Make every effort to keep yourselves united in the Spirit, binding yourselves together with peace. For there is one body and one Spirit, just as you have been called to one glorious hope for the future" (Eph. 4:2–4). The Body of Christ has the same mission and the same blessed future, and if we move toward that future, striving against and looking down at each other, it will not further the cause. It only creates discomfort and delays on the journey. We believers are called to embrace God's spirit of unity and utilize patience and understanding with one another. God does not require more of the believer than He does of Himself. Everyone has their quirks and faults, but that does not call for judgment or criticism. It calls for love and a humble heart that recognizes its weaknesses and handles others with care. We are to put aside our opinions and consider one another, loving one another as God has loved us (John 13:34).

Harmony and Support

One must first know how the Body of Christ functions and acts before they can understand what plagues the Body of Christ. God created the human body with very complex organ systems that help maintain growth, development, and function, and it is the same as the Body of Christ. God designed these systems to work together to operate effectively. Neglect or improper use of any part can cause harm to the Body. Harmony and care among the Body of Christ are essential to its health. We are interconnected, and God placed us here to support, help, and love one another. We are a part of a very vast and intricate whole. However, the vastness of the body does not make one part less significant than all the others. "The human body has many parts, but the many parts make up one whole body. So, it is with the Body of Christ....This makes for harmony among the members so that all the members care for each other. If one part suffers, all the parts suffer with it, and if one part is honored, all the parts are glad. All of you together are Christ's body, and each of you is a part of it" (1 Cor. 12:12, 25–27). Each part of the Body supports and helps the other. Some parts of the Body contribute to more than one system, but when there is an imbalance or when a component does not function properly, the whole body can suffer. Some malfunctions have more encompassing effects than others.

However, all parts of the body are vital and essential to God. Verse 18 in 1 Corinthians says that God placed each person right where He wanted them. He had a reason and plan for giving each individual their particular talents, skills, and experiences so that they could play a role in the Body of Christ. Some like to think they can do it all on their own, but God did not design the church or the body to work that way. When Moses struggled to manage all the tribes' problems on his own, his father-in-law shared the wisdom of delegating responsibilities (Exod. 18). It took days for Moses to accomplish his task because he tried to do everything himself, while thousands of people sat idle, available to help. Those who want to work effectively and make progress in the Body of Christ must find and operate in their proper place.

There is wisdom in sharing the load. God created the body with multiple parts, intending each member to play their role. The body was not designed for a few members to do all the work while the others sit back and receive without contributing anything to further the kingdom. One person or a small group of people should not try to take on all the work of the kingdom but be faithful in the things that God graced them to accomplish. Other members become weak when we do not encourage or allow them to function as they should, just like a muscle that's underutilized and atrophies. Nor should one sit on the sidelines, waiting for others to bear all the load. When we allow others to carry all the burden, they can receive injury, because just like an overused muscle, the strain of the extra load can cause them harm. It can restrict movements and sometimes make it impossible. The body will try to compensate for the overuse or underuse of a part, but if not corrected, the body suffers harm as a whole. There will be times when members of the Body of Christ will need help from the rest of the body, and we should give it. However, assistance should be provided with wisdom and balance. The believer should not live as a parasite, nor should they enable bad social and work habits. We are encouraged in 2 Corinthians 8:13–14 to give others a helping hand so that they can manage their own lives and build themselves up so that they, too, will be in a position to give to others. It also cautions us to be wise in our sharing and not to give to the extent that our lives become difficult while others become easy. Sharing in the Body of God should not be one-directional but done in rotation so that all parts of the Body obtain the kind of support they need.

Be supportive in battle. When the Israelites won the fight against the Amalekites in Exodus 17, it was a group effort. We see Moses as the main character because he leads the people of Israel and has a significant role in determining the outcome of the battle through his obedience to keeping God's staff raised during the fight. However, Moses was not the only one God worked through. Joshua and the army did the actual fighting as Moses held the staff high. Aaron and Hur brought Moses comfort and lent strength when he was tired and no longer strong enough to hold his arms up. All of them working together in doing their part brought about the defeat of their enemy. We win when we function as a unit with the same goal, assisting when needed and not worrying whose name will appear in the limelight.

Cheer for one another. When we see another believer prospering, we should praise God for the blessings that God showers on His children. The crab-in-the-barrow mentality hinders the progress of the Body of Christ. We should want growth and favor for others and not seek to have ours at the expense of another. An impure and adulterous heart delays our blessings (James 4:3–5). God calls for the believer to resist this mentality and come closer to Him. We, as believers, must purify our hearts of the ideology and selfish attitude of this world so that we can be loyal to God's plan for the Body of Christ. We should not cause undue strife in the Body over possessions, opportunities, and other blessings. Instead, we should establish practices that promote unity and peace in the presence of God's blessings.

Summary

   Once we receive God's love by believing in the death and resurrection of His Son, we become a part of the Body of Christ and gain His agenda. We must let the plans and attitudes of the past go and become loyal to what God calls us to do. He wants us as the Body of Christ to be of one mind with many members (Eph. 4:4–10; 1 Pet. 3:8). He has made us all different (looks, talents, tendencies, work ethic, background, mentality) and then unified us by giving us one body, one Spirit, one Lord, one faith, one God and Father. We have the responsibility and privileged to lift, support, and love one another. Our actions and thoughts should promote peace and unity among all members. Daily we encourage ourselves to be considerate, knowing that, when we show compassion and understanding to others, we please God.

God's mandate for unity and peace prepares us to walk patiently and lovingly alongside others rather than in judgment or hatred. Our background, past vices, or loyalties should not be a hindrance to supporting and encouraging others in walking in the abundant life for which Christ died. We have gifts, talents, blessings, and opportunities to not only excel but also build up the Body of Christ around us. The Body of Christ loves and honors God through loving and supporting others. As a Christian in a society that is overly concerned with the validation of feelings and promotion of self, we cannot forget that negative, unrighteous actions are never okay. We are to overcome evil with good, and when we do not take time to respect and consider others, there is a good chance we will walk away from the character and plan of God. Allowing the mentality and arguments of this world to lead us will cause us to reject the dynamics of the Body of Christ, which Christ has established. Christ is the head of the Body, and we should look to Him and His mandates to guide us.

BODY DYNAMICS

Yielding to the Godhead

Some of humanity wants independence from God, not wanting to affiliate with anything other than themselves. However, true freedom from God would mean no breath of life, no purpose, no home, no finances, no relationships. God provides all that can be seen and is unseen to the believer and the nonbeliever. "For he gives his sunlight to both the evil and the good, and he sends rain on the just and the unjust alike" (Matt. 5:45). The unbeliever, like the believer, is dependent on God's mercy and blessings, whether they acknowledge Him or not. He patiently provides, giving those who will recognize Him and receive His love time to do so. Becoming a part of the Body of Christ gives us positions as children, friends, and servants of God. God has done so much for the believer, and we must learn to trust Him, knowing that He only has good intentions toward us (Jeremiah 29:11).

Temples of God. "What? know ye not that your body is the temple of the Holy Ghost, which is in you, which ye have of God, and ye are not your own? For ye are bought with a price: therefore, glorify God in your body, and in your spirit, which are God's" (1 Cor. 6:19–20 KJV). We are here to honor and please

God, and when we do so, we receive blessings for it. A struggle ensues when our desires and will run contrary to what God has established. It may take some practice, but we should get to a place that we willingly yield to what God declares, knowing that it leads to life, healing, growth, and blessings. Striving against God only causes harm by impeding our growth and weakens our stance in things of God.

In this life, our resolve to honor God above our agenda and feelings is continuously tested. God requires faith and obedience from the believer and wants us to learn it on varying levels and in all situations. God is gracious in this, allowing us to take lessons and tests of faith and obedience over and over until passed. He desires that we consult and honor Him while walking through life's journey. Proverbs 16:25 tells us that it is possible to think that something is right and it leads to death. When we walk in conceit, refusing to consult God, believing we know what is best, we can be choosing a path that leads to our demise rather than progressing us in life. Some people have blinding confidence in their knowledge and their earthly wisdom and stake their lives on it, trusting their souls' eternal destination on it. They believe that their analysis of a situation is correct and the plans they devise will succeed. However, the believer should not fall into this trap of the enemy, knowing that earthly wisdom is foolishness to God. The believer should never believe their plans or ways can ever compete with God's. "'My thoughts are nothing like your thoughts,' says the Lord. 'And my ways are far beyond anything you could imagine. For just as the heavens are higher than the earth, so my ways are higher than your ways and my thoughts higher than your thoughts'" (Isa. 55:8–9).

We receive both honor and reward in humility. Humility before God brings strength because one no longer relies on one's strength but the power of God. Striving out of God's will and away from His anointing will get us nowhere, because "the Spirit alone gives eternal life. Human effort accomplishes nothing. And the very words I have spoken to you are spirit and life" (John 6:63). The believer must learn to abide in Christ and be led by the Spirit to function effectively in the Body of Christ. God wants to bless His people and do great things for them and through them. As Creator, He knows our maturity level and the things we can get hung up on, and He blesses us with those things in mind. God wants to prepare and equip us to walk in His abundance and handle our blessings with integrity. He wants to reward the good works of His children in their humility.

He calls us to obedience. Yes, God wants us to have an abundant life filled with milestones and good times. While we are experiencing the abundance of God, we are to be obedient. As it says in 1 Philippians 1:21, "For to me, living means living for Christ and dying is even better." The believer must understand that the Body of Christ is for Christ's purpose, not the desires of all the individual parts. As a part of the body, our priority becomes Christ, and that means honoring Him in life and death. God cares about the believers' needs and desires. When our desires match His will, He will withhold nothing from them. "For the LORD, God is our sun and our shield. He gives us grace and glory. The LORD will withhold no good thing from those who do what is right" (Ps. 84:11). God wants to shine on His people; He wants to protect His people, but when we choose to walk out of His hand and away from His light, we should not expect God's great blessings. God may show grace and mercy to a disobedient believer; however, we receive the full benefits of God in the light of obedience, not in the darkness of rebellion. God has abundant blessings stored up for those who honor and take refuge in Him (Ps. 31:19).

The believer must understand their fragility so they will earnestly embrace wisdom. "Teach us to realize the brevity of life, so that we may grow in wisdom" (Ps. 90:12). Wisdom empowers us to live free of foolish choices and ideas and walk in purpose and the knowledge of God's will. There is a designated amount of time for the Body of Christ to influence this world; let it be a time of reckoning for the enemy and tremendous growth in relationship with God. Lay aside ignorance and opinion and pick up truth and wisdom and exercise them with the authority that God has given. Humanity is clothed in weakness. Sin has corrupted the body that was once eternal. It's now prone to sickness, pain, and death. Humanity has a limited amount of time to experience life and make choices that will affect them and others on this earth. Use the time learning and comprehending the love and Word of God. Let it be spent living life with integrity and helping, supporting, and encouraging others whenever the opportunity presents itself. We use our time wisely when we build up the Body.

Mirroring Christ's Image

Jesus came not only to save the world but also to conform those who believe in Him into His image. When God first created humanity, He made them in His image, and when sin entered the world, it corrupted that image. Through salvation, God wants to restore it. Jesus was an example to the world and to the believers of the character, power, love, and authority that humanity can have if they were to be reborn. Rebirth was not established for humanity to go through and come out the same as if they had not received Christ's redemption. As believers, we are new creatures, and we should leave behind old ways of thinking and habits and establish a righteous way of living through Christ (2 Cor. 5:17). God's grace empowers us to change and act righteously. Our ability to be and do comes from God's grace. We should examine ourselves and ensure that our confidence is not in our ability to sustain a righteous life. The works of Christ make us righteous and empower us to live righteously (Rom. 12:3). Pride and familiarity can cause us to become slack in our duties to follow the character and love of Christ and walk into self-righteousness. We can become fixated on the day-to-day grind of things, forgetting to acknowledge God, our source, and Jesus, our template, for how we should be trying to address living.

Stay Away from Complaining

God disliked complaining in the time of Moses, and He doesn't like it any more today. In 1 Corinthians 10:9–11, Paul writes, "Nor should we put Christ to the test, as some of them did and then died from snakebites. And don't grumble as some of them did, and then were destroyed by the angel of death. These things happened to them as examples for us. They were written down to warn us who live at the end of the age." After all the deliverances, miracles, and provisions God gave the Israelites, they complained. They did not like the avenue in which God chose to bless them, or the timing. God grew tired of their ungratefulness and sent poisonous snakes, and many people died from the snakebites. After this great tragedy and reprimanding, the people of Israel repented and cried out for mercy. God provided a way of healing for them through obedience. He wanted the Israelites to recognize their ungratefulness and repent. Complaining is just that, a show of ungratefulness. Life will bring with it suffering and discomfort. In the trying times of life, God still demands a thankful heart for all the multitude of blessings that He freely provided.

The believer must learn how to be content. Elsewhere, Paul writes, "Not that I was ever in need, for I have learned how to be content with whatever I have. I know how to live on almost nothing or with everything. I have learned the secret of living in every situation, whether it is with a full stomach or empty, with plenty or little. For I can do everything through Christ, who gives me strength" (Phil. 4:11–13). Paul learned how to be satisfied with what he was blessed to have. He learned how to embrace the good times and the not-so-good times because he knew Christ was the source of everything. Paul chose not to complain, knowing that it would take him toward dissatisfaction and lure him into sin. Instead, he looked thankfully to God to provide.

Do not discredit God's blessing through complaining. Complaining and arguing distract from the work of the kingdom. This ungodly practice only gives the world something to point at and say, "Hypocrite." It doesn't solve any problems. It only dishonors God. When we complain, we devalue all the beautiful blessings and miracles that God has freely given us. We diminish our blessings when faced with other disappointments. We should stay busy, bringing light to our situation and encouraging others to look to God for help. We can prevail with hope in the face of disappointment. How can we defend our reason for hoping in Christ if all we do is complain about the life that He has saved and empowered?

> Do everything without complaining and arguing, so that no one can criticize you. Live clean, innocent lives as children of God, shining like bright lights in a world full of crooked and perverse people. Hold firmly to the word of life; then, on the day of Christ's return, I will be proud that I did not run the race in vain and that my work was not useless. (Phi. 2:14–16)

Complaining devalues all that God is doing in you, through you, around you, and for you. Believers do have to deal with disappointment and disagreements, but we should do it with patience, love, and compassion. At times, they may even have to endure longsuffering, but never with complaining.

Complaining and arguing are only a distraction that keeps the believer from walking with purpose: shining Christ's light, living and standing for godliness, proclaiming God's Word, and showing God's love. Unlike complaining, these things make a constructive difference and can bring positive change to our situations.

Forgiveness

The believer is a member of the Body of Christ, but that does not make them perfect or infallible. The Body of Christ consists of imperfect people who are empowered by God to live righteous lives. As the believer grows in Christ, the stumbling blocks and strongholds they face may become easier to overcome, and they may lessen with maturity, but that does not promise they will handle everything righteously and as God has instructed. As believers, we should not hold so tightly to offense and judge others harshly. Colossians 3:13 calls us to "make allowance for each other's faults and forgive anyone who offends you. Remember, the Lord forgave you, so you must forgive others." After becoming a part of the Body of Christ, we should work to make forgiveness and understanding a habit.

God requires the believer to be as forgiving as He is. In Matthew 6, as a part of Jesus's Sermon on the Mount, He tells the crowd that if they refuse to forgive those who have sinned against them, then God would not forgive their sins. In Matthew 18:21–35, Jesus shares a parable of a king's servant who owed the king millions of dollars. The king showed compassion for him, released him, and erased his debt. After being forgiven his debt, he beat up a man who owed him a few silver coins and threw him in prison. When the king heard of the forgiven servant's unwillingness to show mercy after he had received mercy himself, the king ordered that the man be taken and tortured until his debt was repaid. The passage ends with the comment, "That's what my heavenly Father will do to you if you refuse to forgive your brothers and sisters from your heart" (Matt. 5:35). God does not look mercifully on those who received forgiveness and chose to withhold compassion and mercy to others.

Forgiveness does not mean condoning sin. Like 17:3–4 advises us, "So, watch yourselves! If another believer sins, rebuke that person; then, if there is repentance, forgive. Even if that person wrongs you seven times a day and each time turns again and asks forgiveness, you must forgive." When God tells the believer to forgive, it does not mean that one must accept the wrong done to them as right, but it does mean that they must release the anger and weight that came with it so that He can heal and deliver. God is not telling anyone to erase the line between right and wrong; the wrong is to be acknowledged and corrected, yet no matter what the situation, the believer is to forgive. The believer is required to forgive even if for a repeated wrong. God has freely given His forgiveness to those who have sinned against Him, and He wants the believer to do the same. He does not want the weight of past wrongs hindering the believer. Keeping tallies of each person's transgressions against you brings you no benefit, only burden.

Finally, God wants to cleanse and build up the believer, not condemn them. As it says in 1 John 1:9, "But if we confess our sins to him, he is faithful and just to forgive us our sins and to cleanse us from all wickedness." God wants the believer to acknowledge their wrong so that He can purify them of their wrongdoings. Our soul is like our clothes; we can start the day with them clean and pressed, but we may acquire stains, marks, debris, and odors throughout the day. We have varying degrees of success as we try to honor God each day. Some days we reach the end with just a smudge here and there. On other days, we look as if we had wrestled in the mud. Whatever the case, we usually have some degree of filth that we need to wash away at the end of the day. It is the same with our souls. We should not go through life thinking that living with stains, tears, and filth is okay when we have Christ. We should go through the day repenting and cleansing our souls. We should wash our hands. God wants continuous and free-flowing communion and relationship with the believer, and He provides the believer a way to approach Him and not be turned away, and that is through repentance. Ephesians 5:25–27 says thus:

> He gave up his life for her to make her holy and clean, washed by the cleansing of God's Word. He did this to present her to himself as a glorious church without a spot or wrinkle or any other blemish. Instead, she will be holy and without fault.

As members of the Body of Christ, we should work with God and take advantage of repentance so that we can present ourselves to Him without spot or wrinkle. Why dishonor God with the stench of sin when He has provided us with soap and water for our souls at a high cost?

Summary

As believers and members of the Body of Christ, we must understand that God is the head and will always be the head. His agenda of love, peace, unity, and forgiveness will not change, and it is more important than any other plan that flesh or the world can come up with, and it should become our priority. God made the body to honor Him by becoming like Him, and we must fight against the tendency to sway from God's principles and maintain the resolve to look to God for strength and companionship to walk this journey with gratefulness and contentment in His will.

Our intellect, resources, and skills all come from God. Believing that we know better or have something unique to offer outside of Him only keeps us from truly experiencing God and growing in the grace that He provides. God will give us continuous instruction because we need it. We will never experience enough, read enough, receive enough of God's Word to reach the mark of perfection on this earth. However, we can find peace and purpose in walking in the will of God now. With joy and patience, we must learn to embrace the principles of God and identify the social norms and individual inclinations that will try to hinder us from walking in the grace of God and becoming more like Christ.

The wisdom, resources, character, and opportunities we need to be successful in the now stages and future stages of life all come from God. For us to be successful in the presence of all these provisions, we need to become good stewards establishing good health practices and maintaining them.

HYGIENE *and* MAINTENANCE

Hygiene is vital to getting well and staying healthy. Our soul needs care just like our physical bodies, and we need to establish and maintain practices that will allow for healing and growth in every part of our being. We must protect ourselves against negative influences and guard ourselves against creating bad habits. We can do this through good spiritual hygiene. The World Health Organization defines hygiene as "conditions or practices that help to maintain health and prevent the spread of disease." For the Body of Christ to maintain health among the believers and not pass on harmful practices and mentalities, we must exercise spiritual hygiene to avoid sickness in this depraved and dying world. Once we learn spiritual hygiene practices, they must be maintained to preserve health.

Good spiritual practices plant us in fertile soil for growth and development. When establishing habits that draw us closer to God and emulate Christ, we guard ourselves against the influence of temptations of this world. The believer must work diligently with Christ to stay clean and healthy, putting forth an effort to walk in the character and the calling of God.

By staying consistent in healthy spiritual practices such as praying, studying God's Word, and fellowshipping with other believers (1 Tim. 4:13, 15–16), we can avoid many of the pitfalls the enemy places in our path. While trying to maintain a spiritually healthy lifestyle, we must acknowledge the possible pitfalls and stumbling blocks that occur on life's journey.

While establishing good practices, we must remember that the enemy does not cheer us on in our efforts but instead tries to distract, frustrate, and hinder. The enemy likes to encourage believers toward sloppiness and inconsistency in their spiritual hygiene practices through temptation. The believer must understand that temptation does not come from the outside but from within themselves. "Temptation comes from our own desires, which entice us and drag us away. These desires give birth to sinful actions. And when sin is allowed to grow, it gives birth to death" (James 1:12–15). One of our greatest struggles is with ourselves, and Satan capitalizes on it, using desires to gain ground in our thoughts and decision-making. It is helpful and an excellent preventative measure to acknowledge the things that entice us and praying for God's wisdom and help to handle and overcome them. Unrighteous desires are seeds that, once watered with opportunity and time, will continuously grow until they are pulled out by the root and discarded for the toxic thoughts that they are. When we acknowledge that our thoughts are traveling a wrong road, we have the power to refuse the trip that would lead us to sin. We should do as Paul advised and change the focus of our thoughts and think on true, noble, right, and simple things

(Phil. 4:8). When our mind meditates on these good things, sinful desires have less opportunity to grow into sin because we are not feeding into the urge. We resist, and instead, we nurture seeds of righteousness.

Another critical practice for spiritual hygiene is repentance. Psalm 32 reminds us that not repenting can cause not only mental sickness but also physical sickness: "When I refused to confess my sin, my body wasted away, and I groaned all day long" (Ps. 32:3). The believer must make a habit of confessing one's sin. Whether they considered their transgression large or small, disobedience and rebellion are still disobedience and rebellion to God. God's dislike of sin does not cause disease in the believer; sin is the disease because it is foreign to the original design and purpose of God, and it causes decay and illness spiritually and physically. Sin itself is sickness, and when the believer sins, its side effects manifest in our souls—our minds—and, sometimes, in our physical bodies. The believer should be quick to examine oneself and repent. "Sin is no longer your master, for you no longer live under the requirements of the law. Instead, you live under the freedom of God's grace" (Rom. 6:14). Sin does not control us, so we should not allow it to lead our lives. We have been empowered through God's grace to live righteously.

Heart Change

We must learn to choose a change of heart over self-denial. When trying to maintain a healthy lifestyle, we must not take the route of self-deprivation but one of transformation.

As believers, the self-help lifestyle our society buys into will not bring about the necessary changes of heart to maintain a righteous living. There are several helpful tips out there, but none have the power to transform one's life in a way that eternally matters or brings spiritual deliverance or healing. Being saved is about more than just practices and regiments. It is about a relationship with God. While in we are a relationship with Him, He helps us become more like His Son, which is not a change we can make on our own. Self-deprivation and stringent rules take only the pleasure from our lives, not the desire from our hearts. God wants to cleanse the soul and bring actual healing and strength to the believer. He does not want to lead them from one state of bondage to another.

> You have died with Christ, and he has set you free from the spiritual powers of this world. So why do you keep on following the rules of the world, such as, "Don't handle! Don't taste! Don't touch!"? Such rules are mere human teachings about things that deteriorate as we use them. These rules may seem wise because they require strong devotion, pious self-denial, and severe bodily discipline. But they provide no help in conquering a person's evil desires. (Col. 2:20–23)

Chapter 3 follows this with a call to put to death the sin that lurks within us. Self-control is essential to keeping us from getting carried into sin by the flow of unchecked emotions, desires, and actions. God gave us feelings and desires so that we could intimately experience, embrace, and enjoy life. The enemy perverts the blessings of God by using our feeling to drive us toward desiring wicked things. Wisdom and self-control enable us to identify and adequately handle unrighteous desires and mentalities. Christ said that He came so that we "might have life and have it more abundantly." Does that sound like it calls for self-deprivation? God is calling believers to yield our hearts to being cleansed so that His Spirit can work in and through us until the unrighteous desires no longer have prime placement in our hearts. To gain control over these desires, we must first acknowledge their presence and then ask God to help us make a change.

Practices

To maintain good health within the body, we must practice interacting with one another as the Word of God lays out. The believer should commune with the rest of the body. The other parts give strength, support, and encouragement. Who best to minister to one another than those who know the power, promise, and peace of God? The enemy tries to isolate the believer mentally, if not physically. Satan understands the strength that can be found in groups and knows that if he can get a believer alone, he has a better chance of wearing down an individual's will. If no one is there to encourage and strengthen the believer with God's truths and promises, the believer has to fight off the enemy's attacks by themselves. But they do not have to go at it alone. Just as predators target the strays of the herd, the enemy targets the isolated believer.

As a part of a community, we are to assemble in unity and encourage one another to do good works. We have an allotted amount of time to make an impact on this word. Let's utilize one another and work together with excellence and wisdom to accomplish our common goal. There is strength found in numbers and support found within the community of believers.

> Let us think of ways to motivate one another to acts of love and good works. And let us not neglect our meeting together, as some people do, but encourage one another, especially now that the day of his return is drawing near. (Heb. 10:24–25)

Believers are responsible not only to love but also to correct in love. When we come together, we make ourselves accountable to one another, and we encourage one another to walk the narrow path with more integrity. While trying to come together as the Body, we should not invite in sinful mentalities under the guise of tolerance. We should always show love to people, but we should not pretend that wrong is right because someone chooses to walk out of the will of God. When we do this, we wrongfully stamp approval on something that weaker saints or less knowledgeable people do not know to avoid. We may encourage them to associate with a situation that causes them unnecessary struggle or harm.

There will be many instances that cause believers to stray, and God wants us to recognize them so that we can quickly return to Him. However, if one refuses to correct their behavior, they become an impediment to the Body. The Word instructs us to pray for wayward believers and to allow them to walk away from the rest of the body so as not to corrupt the other parts. After the Body has done its part and acknowledging the wrong in love and opening the door to reconciliation, rejection of repentance leaves the body with only one healthy choice—removing the infected and sinning believer. They must lead the wayward believer to God's methods of discipline; He knows how best to deal with them. The body does not necessarily lose its love for that member. Instead, they step back in love and wisdom and allow God to discipline while they pray for this member's deliverance as if they were "a pagan or a corrupt tax collector." In 1 Corinthians 5:5, the Word says, "Then you must throw this man out and hand him over to Satan so that his sinful nature will be destroyed and he will be saved on the day the Lord returns." God corrects those He loves, and some souls choose to take a more severe route of correction because of stubbornness, but it does not change God's commitment to their salvation. We are responsible for taking care of and ministering to parts of the Body of Christ that are hurting or malfunctioning. To maintain wellness, we have to address those areas in our lives that have been influenced or controlled by sin.

Walk in your given authority. God provides the believer with the authority to speak on His behalf so that we can command change in our lives and the lives of others. We can speak into existence those things that align with His will for us. Jesus lets us know the perimeters and the how-to of the authority given us. "I tell you the truth, whatever you forbid on earth will be forbidden in heaven, and whatever you permit on earth will be permitted in heaven" (Matt. 18:18). When we proclaim those things that God has implemented in heaven, we are releasing the manifestation of God's will on this earth. When confronting something that opposes the will of God, we have the authority to call it into alignment with the will and Word of God. We received the power of Jesus's name to speak the will of God into this earth. We can know the will of God through His Word and Spirit. When we talk to God's will, our authority is validated, and we see the will of God manifested in our lives.

Operate in wisdom and not just gifts. God blessed each part of the body with gifts and talents to edify the Body and bring sinners to repentance. The believer can use those talents and gifts at their discretion, but immaturity or ego may cause them to use them unproductively. We have gifts and talents to benefit others. Paul tells us that "a spiritual gift is given to each of us so we can help each other" (1 Cor. 12:7). The spiritual gifts and talents that God blessed each believer will not be the same, but it will be distributed to each believer as the Holy Spirit sees fit. When God gives us a gift, we are responsible for using it wisely. The Holy Spirit guides us in the proper way and time to utilize our gifts, and we should yield to His leading. However, we can use spiritual gifts outside of God's intended purpose.

In 1 Corinthians 14, Paul lets us know that there are times and places to use our gifts and we should take the time to look at the situation and environment and discern what will be beneficial, not a stumbling block to others. The believer is to be blameless when it comes to evil things but knowledgeable about the things of God (1 Cor. 14:20). Don't squander the gifts of God by not learning about them and growing in them so that we can handle them properly. Take time to understand the power and purpose of your gifts. God has blessed the body with many gifts, and they should be understood, exercised, and used in manners beneficial to the Body of Christ.

God gives us gifts to bring about unity, not division or hierarchies. He has given us not only skills, talents, and abilities but also a ministry. "Now these are the gifts Christ gave to the church: the apostles, the prophets, the evangelists, and the pastors and teachers. Their responsibility is to equip God's people to do his work and build up the church, the Body of Christ" (Eph. 4:11–12). We have been purposed and equipped to be contributing members of the body.

> I appeal to you, dear brothers and sisters, by the authority of our Lord Jesus Christ, to live in harmony with each other. Let there be no divisions in the church. Rather, be of one mind, united in thought and purpose. (1 Cor. 1:10)

Work toward harmony and unity. Harmony among the Body of Christ is essential; it allows the members to function properly with one another, working without contention to reach common goals: health, growth, love, and relationship. Jesus prayed for the Body in John 17:23: "I am in them, and you are in me. May they experience such perfect unity that the world will know that you sent me and that you love them as much as you love me." Jesus wanted the Body to understand and practice unity. The saying "A house divided" holds. It is impossible to keep many moving parts together if all they want to do is push and pull away from one another. Jesus desires unity and harmony for the Body, and the Word of God continuously reminds us of it: "Do all that you can to live in peace with everyone" (Rom. 12:18). God encourages the believer to live in unity because chaos and confusion are the enemy's playgrounds. As Paul says in 1 Corinthians 14:33, "God is not a God of disorder but of peace." The unity of the Body allows the world to see God's love, and when we allow confusion and discord in, we only provide a stage for Satan and his works.

Psalm 133:1 gives a simple and straightforward reason to strive toward unity: it is simply more pleasant and enjoyable to live in harmony rather than disagreement and contention. The believer should try with every effort to stay united with the Body, living together in peace (Eph. 4:3). The Body has many unique individuals, and it is more durable and can accomplish much more in unity. Unity provides a synchronized atmosphere that allows the believer to live and worship more freely, away from confusion and discord.

God gave the members of the Body gifts to strengthen and unify it. He created us to live and work together toward a common goal. He gave us different ministries and gifts to promote, develop, and educate the Body so that it may grow in maturity. Each believer is in a different stage of growth, but when one does not embrace the teaching and ministering of the Body, they stunt their growth. Stunted growth is not healthy in any developmental cycle. When a believer allows ignorance, fleshly comfort, or disobedience to cause discord among the Body, they no longer move forward in the will of God in that area but are stagnated in rebellion. Friction affects the flow of ministry, and some of the members can flow around it like a flowing river moves around a branch or debris, while other members get stuck behind them—unity of the faith is a sign of maturity.

Unity is hard when one cannot lay down their opinions and desires. We must learn that the will of God and the betterment of others are more important than our judgment and comfort. Paul reminds us in Romans 12:16 that the key to unity is humility: "Live in harmony with each other. Don't be too proud to enjoy the company of ordinary people. And don't think you know it all!" The Word of God continuously discusses humility and its benefits because the love of self can cause discord and restlessness. It causes selective blindness so that a person only sees what benefits them. When you put aside what you think you know and take the time to engage and understand others, you can begin to see a bigger picture. Not only do you see a bigger picture, but you can also enjoy being a part of it.

Summary

Maintaining healthy spiritual practices allows the believer to heal and stay spiritually healthy. We must allow God to deal with our hearts and change our lifestyles to see the healing and growth that God desires for each of us. We must implement practices that help us avoid the enemy's traps. God wants unity and harmony among the Body of Christ, and we must be willing to understand and love others to accomplish this harmony. God wants to lead us into practices that help us focus on healthy practices. These practices are not laws, and they are not supposed to bring stress or frustration to the believer. Their purpose is deliverance and growth. God wants to minister to the believer and change their heart so that they can make wise choices. Prayer, mediation, and Bible study are other practices utilized to help maintain a healthy lifestyle and are discussed in more detail in the chapters "Communication" and "Dedication." Living out our faith is more than establishing physical disciplines to keep us from sinning. It requires a change of heart so that we can handle life and perform God's purpose contentedly.

FUNCTIONING PROPERLY

God blessed each individual with various gifts, skills, knowledge, and opportunities. He gave them so we can sustain ourselves in our growth and to contribute to the Body of Christ. God empowers us through His Spirit to do mighty things not only in our lives but also in the lives of others. He encourages us to grow and use these gifts, not to place them on a shelf to be admired or shoved in a closet to be forgotten. He gives us these resources so that we can walk effectively in our purpose. While we endeavor to love God, we are also to love others. God has placed us in families, communities, and churches so that we have plenty of opportunities to put that love into action. When we do not act out our mandate to love, we are not functioning correctly. A malfunctioning part hinders any system or machine from accomplishing its purpose. When we go about life and choose not to honor the principles and standards of God, we become a malfunctioning part of the system that can cause frustration, disappointment, and in some instances, harm.

Productivity

God wants us to utilize His resources responsibly to support the Body. He does not want us to hoard, waste, or exploit them. Matthew 25 shares the parable of the three servants who were entrusted with bags of currency. Two of the servants put the money to good use and gained more for their master, while one buried the money he was given. The servant's excuse was that he did not want to lose the master's investment because he feared punishment. He knew the master was known for amassing great wealth from many avenues and feared that he would fail. The master did not buy into this servant's excuses. Verses 26 and 27 in the chapter convey the master's reply, "You wicked and lazy servant! If you knew I harvested crops I didn't plant and gathered crops I didn't cultivate, why didn't you deposit my money in the bank? At least I could have gotten some interest on it." The master saw through the servant's deceived mind and shared a simple and sure way that he could have made his portion profitable if he had just applied himself. Whether it was actual fear or just plain laziness, the servant had avenues that would not put him in jeopardy of losing the master's money. God's graciousness delegitimizes any believer's excuse for squandering the gifts that He has given: "Never be lazy but work hard and serve the Lord enthusiastically" (Rom. 12:11).

God looks for us not to appear productive but to place actual effort toward the things He deems important. Busyness does not equal God-purposed productivity. For example, consider the fig tree that was leafy but bore no fruit when Jesus went to eat from it. It looked pretty and healthy but did not perform its purpose, which was to produce figs, so Christ cursed the tree (Matt. 11:12–14). If we do not produce the fruit of His Spirit (Gal. 5:22–23), we are not productive. In 3 John, John reveals to us that God wants us to prosper in our everyday endeavors as we prosper spiritually. We are on the right track for achieving this when we walk in truth and treat others kindly. Right after the passage about the fig tree, Jesus turns over tables, reprimanding vendors and preventing the sale of goods in God's temple. This reaction demonstrates that God is not only displeased with unproductivity when it is time for harvest but that He also does not tolerate the misuse and abuse of His temple. As believers, we are His temple, which means we should put aside unrighteous practices and live in a manner that shares God's love and the good news.

Paul was ready to see death because he had done his part on earth and was ready to receive his reward. While Paul was on this earth, he wanted to be useful. He committed himself to his purpose, but he knew that once he was done, he would be ready to die (Heb. 4:10). For us that are still here, we should long to hear, "Well done, my good and faithful servant. You have been faithful in handling this small amount, so now I will give you many more responsibilities. Let's celebrate together!" (Matt. 25:23). Each believer must determine if this will be their resolve. Will they walk in the things of God with diligence so that they will be recognized and rewarded as good and faithful servants? Or will they be disciplined by God because of laziness or their unwillingness to trust God enough to walk with Him in purpose?

Stewardship

Believers are stewards of God's gifts and blessings, and we must take this responsibility seriously (Rom. 12:6–8). The blessings of God can have an enormous impact or little to no impact, depending on how we nurture and utilize them. The first book of Corinthians 12:7 tells us that the purpose of spiritual gifts is so that the different parts of the Body can help one another. In 1 Timothy, Paul writes words of encouragement and instructions to Timothy, a minister of the gospel. In chapter 4, verses 14–16, he encourages Timothy not to neglect the spiritual gifts that he has received. Timothy is instructed to be diligent with his gifts and throw himself into God's purpose for His life. Paul also teaches him to avoid veering from the path of righteousness and to be mindful of how he lives and shares the gospel. He advises him to consider his salvation and the salvation of those around him. With salvation comes responsibility and help to fulfill those responsibilities. The second book of Corinthians 4:7 tells us that "we now have this light shining in our hearts, but we ourselves are like fragile clay jars containing this great treasure. This makes it clear that our great power is from God, not from ourselves" (2 Cor. 4:7). Yes, the believer is human and fragile, but God does not expect the believer to influence the people around them from their strength. He has placed His Spirit within the believer, and He is the one that shines through the life of the believer to bring light where there was once darkness and power where there used to be only oppression. The believer should never allow themselves to think that what they have accomplished is of their might: all is a gift and blessing from God. He chose each believer as a vessel to show the world His love and power.

We are to be good stewards of the instructions and opportunities that God gives us (1 Cor. 4:2). Sometimes the believer may hesitate to follow the Spirit's lead due to fear, laziness, pride, or ignorance. God has a purpose and a goal, and He will navigate us to them and help us fulfill them if we allow Him. Any reason to not follow and disobey is inadequate and only masks itself as logical thinking. God has a purpose for what He calls us to do. Through our obedience, we honor His wisdom and place our faith in Him.

Obedience vs. a Good Plan

Believers do not need to know everything to follow instructions when they are faithful, because they know that He who has given the instructions is faithful and just. God has a purpose for His teachings and the gifts He gives, and the believer does not have to know intricate details to obey. Has someone ever asked you for help while they were fixing something? They say, "Hold this," "Pass that," or "Push this"; they don't go into detail. They just need you to do as they ask so that they can complete their task. Sometimes God allows the believer to see immediately how their actions affect their lives and the lives of others. If He does not, it doesn't change what He calls us to do or the impact it will make. Wisdom is not about knowing everything; it's about having the ability to judge and apply the knowledge that you do have. When faced with situations you do not quite understand, use wisdom to call on that which you do know of God's Word and use good judgment to walk in obedience.

Obedience requires the believer to do more than follow instructions. God knows what He wants, and He doesn't need the believer reinterpreting His will. When God determined it was time to fulfill His promise to Moses and take vengeance on the Amalekites, He chose King Saul to do it. God spoke to the prophet Samuel, and Samuel conveyed God's plan to Saul and Saul's role in that plan: "This is what the LORD of Heaven's Armies has declared: I have decided to settle accounts with the nation of Amalek for opposing Israel when they came from Egypt. Now go and completely destroy the entire Amalekite nation—men, women, children, babies, cattle, sheep, goats, camels, and donkeys" (1 Sam. 15:2). Samuel tells Saul precisely what to do and why God wants it done. In Exodus 17:14, after the Israelites defeated the Amalekites, God tells Moses that He is going to wipe the Amalekites off the face of the earth. When Samuel goes to Saul, we see God's intention to follow through on that promise. However, Saul deviated from the plan and "spared Agag's life and kept the best of the sheep and goats, the cattle, the fat calves, and the lambs—everything that appealed to them. They destroyed what was worthless or of poor quality" (1 Sam. 15:9). Saul disobeyed God by sparing the king and the good livestock.

Our disobedience displeases God, and it has consequences. God's response to Saul's rebellion was in verse 11: "I am sorry that I ever made Saul king, for he has not been loyal to me and has refused to obey my command." When Samuel confronts him, Saul seems oblivious to the fact that God is angry with him. He describes how he did what the Lord said and spared the king and livestock. Saul focused more on his success and the things that He had gained that he was unwilling to acknowledge his unfaithfulness to God and His plan. In verses 22–23, Samuel replies to Saul's indifference, "What is more pleasing to the LORD: your burnt offerings and sacrifices or your obedience to his voice? Listen! Obedience is better than sacrifice, and submission is better than offering the fat of rams. Rebellion is as sinful as witchcraft, and stubbornness as bad as worshiping idols. So, because you have rejected the command of the LORD, he has rejected you as king." God took away Saul's anointing as king because He could not manage it faithfully.

Being Faithful

We do not have to understand the Holy Spirit's rationale for the distribution of gifts, but we do need to honor His choices. God distributed gifts according to his wisdom, and His choices should be respected. We should not envy another believer for their gifts. We should instead embrace them and receive how God is blessing the Body through them. By staying unified and grateful for God's blessing, no matter how they are distributed, we glorify and honor God. God wants to see what each believer will do with what He has given them, just like the parable of the three servants, and He will bless them with more if they can be faithful with what they have received.

If we cannot value the gifts and skills that we already have, we set ourselves up for discontent. Faithfulness calls us to constancy, and when we waver in our contentment, we begin to slack in our commitment. Change and novelty (a new <u>fill in the blank</u>) do not remedy an ungrateful or discontented heart. It is rectified through gratefulness for the present and recognition of the value in the now. When we receive blessings of new relationships, resources, opportunities, or positions, an ungrateful attitude can overshadow the excitement of its newness and make it a reason for discontent. God blesses those who are faithful. Faithful not only to the mountaintop experiences but also trust Him and enjoy life with Him in the valleys and on the mountainsides.

Give on Your Level

We are to be more than just a receiver of His blessings but also a sower. God wants the believer to give cheerfully, honoring those who give generously by allowing them to reap bountifully (2 Cor. 9:6–7). The events leading up to Ananias's and Sapphira's reveal that God does not look strictly at what we offer but at our heart when we give. In Act 5:3–5, Peter asks, "'Ananias, why have you let Satan fill your heart? You lied to the Holy Spirit, and you kept some of the money for yourself. The property was yours to sell or not sell, as you wished. And after selling it, the money was also yours to give away. How could you do a thing like this? You weren't lying to us but to God!' As soon as Ananias heard these words, he fell to the floor and died. Everyone who heard about it was terrified." Ananias and

Sapphira thought more about how people would view them than how their deceitful hearts would insult and displease God. God freely gives to us, and He would like for us to give back graciously. We do not need to disillusion ourselves or deceive others so that we appear well in their eyes. If we have an issue with giving, then we should pray about it, asking God to help us in this area. We should not allow ungracious and sour attitudes to linger, because they will only suck the life and joy out of walking faithfully with Christ. When we see are heart waning, we should seek God's help to strengthen and deliver us so that we can move beyond those stumbling blocks that discourage us from sowing into the lives of others. We should meet the needs of the church at what level we are until they receive freedom and faith to do or give on another level.

We must operate in love. Using the principles of love as our guide enables us to please God with our giving. In 1 Corinthians 13:3 we are told, "If I gave everything I have to the poor and even sacrificed my body, I could boast about it; but if I didn't love others, I would have gained nothing." God cares more about the condition of one's heart than the status of a bank account or how many "good deeds" someone accumulates. God is not a business or institution that cares only about the bottom line or the amount of work done. God cares about the person, and He wants them to be in a decent place. God wants the believer to enjoy their walk with Him and lovingly embrace their purpose and His people. The world will know that the believer is a child of God through their love, and if the believer struggles to walk in love, they may need to examine why. We need to learn to release resentment and embrace forgiveness so that we can indeed operate in love. Sometimes we need to re-evaluate our actions to see if they are wrong for us. God does not always ordain every opportunity to do a good deed or act. The believer should pray about what they participate in and what occupies their time and thoughts. If the believer acts out of obligation, guilt, or another pressure, they may deviate from love. When there is a love issue, it comes from a heart issue. And we should take it seriously and place it before God to clean and heal.

Eyes on the Kingdom, Not the Blessings

God desires to provide the believer with everything they need. We should not fret over the resources in our lives if we trust in God and walk in His will. Matthew 6:33 advises us to "seek the Kingdom of God above all else, and live righteously, and he will give you everything you need." Seeking God's kingdom first does not mean that we should discard our earthly responsibilities. We are to ask God for the direction of our lives and then handle our worldly responsibilities using His wisdom and provision. Issues arise when we set aside nurturing our relationship with God and only pursue material things. Jesus shares a parable in Luke 12:16–21 to warn the believer about setting wrong priorities. A rich man who amasses wealth dies before he can enjoy his bounty. The man may have accumulated great wealth on earth but was not rich in his relationship with God. He prioritized profit, and it occupied all his days. In his quest for a comfortable retirement, he put little or no time and effort into his relationship with God. When He finally decided to enjoy the fruits of his labor, his time on this earth was at its end, so his lifelong efforts were in vain. He placed his efforts strictly on gaining earthly wealth. He decided not to prioritize his relationship with the Creator of it all.

God called the believer to prioritize Him in their lives, and He should always fit into the equation. The believer ought to live for the Source, not just the resources. God is there for the believer and provides what is needed and even what is wanted; however, we are unwise only to pursue materialistic and finite, temporal things. Matthew 6:19–21 tells us, "Don't store up treasures here on earth, where moths eat them and rust destroys them, and where thieves break in and steal. Store your treasures in heaven, where moths and rust cannot destroy, and thieves do not break in and steal. Wherever your treasure is, there, the desires of your heart will also be." We should place our attention and energy on nurturing our relationship with God. We should allow His Holy Spirit to guide and equip us, for these are the things that will last for eternity, not material wealth, which gives way to age and decay.

Summary

A clean heart and a renewed mind prepare us to function properly. God is calling us to an essential and valuable commitment. It is a work of the heart, not just of resources. He wants us to be engaged and have good relationships with one another so that we can come together and handle life in a way that prospers us all. The Body of Christ is a community. We have to care for one another and get along for our community to thrive. When we are kingdom-minded, we see the need for participation and dedication so that all can benefit and grow. God calls us to certain things because He knows the importance of them to the health of us individually and that of the Body of Christ. When we actively participate as a unit trying not only to look good but also make a difference, we can stay consistent in our productivity, stewardship, obedience, faithfulness, and giving. God wants His believers to do more than just fight the enemy. When we work together and utilize the gifts, tools, wisdom, and principles of God in our lives, we give the enemy less ground and opportunity to operate. He will continuously come up against the Body of Christ and our unity. Still, when we work together and suit up with the tools that God has provided, life becomes more enjoyable, less of a war zone that continually has us anxious, weary, and overwhelmed. When there are unity and commitment to the same God-ordained goals, we can walk in the peace and joy of God.

PROPER ATTIRE

God provides the Body of Christ with protection so that we can stand in the freedom that Christ has given us. God gave us a set of armor for defense against the attacks of the enemy. We also have this armor so that we can come against the camp of the enemy. The armor of God is made of the foundational truths of salvation and relationship with Christ. When we wear them, we are prepared to handle each situation, emotion, personality, and attack we may face throughout our day. Wearing these truths not only protects us but also gives us reassurance in who we are and what we have and do in Christ. We should not set the weapons that God has given us, thinking we will not need them. God gave them to us because they are required to walk this life in victory. We need to understand the truths that the armor of God holds and the protection it provides so that we can use them properly against the devices of the enemy. We must wear all the parts of the armor so that we are not left vulnerable. The armor of God and His tools are the only things effective against the attacks and weapons of the enemy.

Ephesians 6:13–17 lets us know God has given us this armor so that we can stand firm as we fight and defend our faith. God has given us tools to protect our freedom in Christ and live life victoriously.

Therefore, put on every piece of God's armor so you will be able to resist the enemy in the time of evil. Then after the battle, you will still be standing firm. Stand your ground, putting on the belt of truth and the body armor of God's righteousness. For shoes, put on the peace that comes from the good news so that you will be fully prepared. In addition to all these, hold up the shield of faith to stop the fiery arrows of the devil. Put on salvation as your helmet, and take the sword of the Spirit, which is the Word of God. Pray in the Spirit at all times and on every occasion. Stay alert and be persistent in your prayers for all believers everywhere (Eph. 6:13–17).

Belt of Truth

The belt of truth secures the armor and gives the believer a place to store and secure their weapons for battle. The truth keeps the believer battle-ready, whether for self-defense or to overcome the enemy. Jesus is the source of truth and provides the way to God and eternal life (John 14:6). The enemy confronted Jesus after His fast and tried to undermine the will of God. Jesus did not try to come up with new concepts or principles to fight the enemy but used what had been established by God. He used the words, will, and truth of God to withstand the attacks of the enemy. We should use what has been given to us by God to confront and overcome the enemy in our daily walk.

How does truth work? "And you will know the truth, and the truth will set you free" (John 8:32). The believer must know the Word of God for it to have an impact on our lives. Without knowledge of the Scripture, we cower in the face of confrontation rather than tap into the Spirit and use the power, love, and self-discipline that God gives us. Knowledge of the truth prevents the enemy from deceiving the believer (Acts 17:11). Understanding the Word for ourselves allows us to knowledgeably agree with it when it is expressed or spoken and wisely discard those words and actions that do not align with God's standards.

The instrument of truth. "When the Spirit of truth comes, he will guide you into all truth. He will not speak on his own but will tell you what he has heard. He will tell you about the future" (John 16:13). The Spirit that God placed in the believer upon salvation helps the believer navigate in their walk. He helps us to understand the truth and apply it to our lives. He guides us in the things of God. The Spirit of God never contradicts the Word of God, so if a thought or voice opposes the Word of God, we should resist and rebuke it. If someone tells you to condone or participate in any kind of sin, you know to refuse the suggestion because it is not from God. If you have thoughts of unworthiness, you know to discard those thoughts because they are not from God. God's Spirit is not going to contradict His Word, so we should not receive any thought, idea, or suggestions that holds a contradictory meaning to God's Word. We should reject and discard them.

Purpose of truth. "Make them holy by your truth; teach them your word, which is truth" (John 17:17). The truth of the Word of God cleanses the believer and brings us to a standard of moral and spiritual excellence. The truth continually works on the believer. It peels and removes earthly attitudes and opinions, and it replaces them with the character, words, and principles of God. The truth also preserves the believer, keeping us away from the tricks and traps of the enemy. As it says in Psalms 40:11, "Withhold not thou thy tender mercies from me, O LORD: let thy lovingkindness and thy truth continually preserve me." When the believer knows the truth, they can more readily spot the lies of the enemy, avoiding the pitfalls of pride, poor self-image, and the enticement to sin.

Application of truth. "Keep their words always in your heart. Tie them around your neck. When you walk, their counsel will lead you. When you sleep, they will protect you. When you wake up, they will advise you. For their command is a lamp and their instruction a light; their corrective discipline is the way to life" (Prov. 6:21–23). The truth is not something the believer should only recall in time of oppression and struggle, but we should also apply the Word of God all the time in every area of our lives. We should wear truth like a cherished pendant around the neck, kept close during every activity of the day. We should take it with us everywhere and feel its absence when we stray from its wisdom. We must remember the importance of truth: it leads, protects, and advises the believer. God's word shines a light on issues and should be shared with others so that they, too, can receive a revelation of their situations and receive wisdom on how to walk in the freedom that Christ so graciously offers.

Breastplate of Righteousness

In the face of God, the Just Judge, humanity is guilty, and the enemy, the accuser of the Body of Christ, cries out for justice. He proclaims that we have no right to anything but judgment and sentencing. When we received the works of Christ, we received His righteousness, and it covers our faults and sins, and God declares us right. Christ's righteousness is the only thing that makes us right before God and makes the enemy's accusations ungrounded in our lives, in the eyes of God. Christ did more than just pay off humanity's debt of sin; He rebirthed us into a state wherein we can have a relationship with God and house God's Spirit, and that happened when He gave us His righteousness. The breastplate of righteousness covers the believer, protecting all that is vital to the believer's relationship with God, and defends the enemy's fiery darts of accusations against the believer.

Dedication and self-discipline are great tools, but without first acknowledging the need for Christ's righteousness and receiving it, they are powerless. Self-righteousness will not hold up against sin and its corrupt nature. When we try to grow and succeed on our own, we omit the Spirit and power of God that empower us to grow and succeed righteously in our walk with Christ. Self-righteousness feeds a mentality that encourages us to lean and depend on ourselves, not God. Paul tells us this:

Everything else is worthless when compared with the infinite value of knowing Christ Jesus, my Lord. For his sake, I have discarded everything else, counting it all as garbage, so that I could gain Christ and become one with him. I no longer count on my own righteousness through obeying the law; rather, I become righteous through faith in Christ. For God's way of making us right with himself depends on faith. (Phil. 3:9)

The believer should do all things with the knowledge that God blessed them with those capabilities. The breastplate of righteousness relieves the believer from the frustration and futility that accompany works of the flesh.

Shoes of Peace: Good News

The gospel of peace is reassurance that God fulfilled His promise and that Christ's birth, death, burial, and resurrection paid the debt of our sin and bought about our deliverance from sin's control. The believer can be confident in their salvation without worrying about what we can do to be disinherited by God. When we wear the shoes of the good news, we walk at peace with God, praising and glorifying Him. We walk knowing that because of salvation, the Spirit of God keeps us until the day of redemption. We are secure in God's love, even in the face of sin and unrighteous circumstances. God is faithful and just to forgive us and walk us toward healing and deliverance.

The good news defends against the uncertainties about the security of our relationship with God. The good news proclaims the love and extent to which God went to receive us into His arms and family. The good news is also an offensive tool used to reclaim ground that the enemy has stolen. "These were his instructions to them: 'The harvest is great, but the workers are few. So, pray to the Lord, who is in charge of the harvest; ask him to send more workers into his fields'" (Luke 10:2). There are a lot of souls out there to recover and invite into the kingdom of God, and God gave us the good news as a tool to draw them. We must walk prepared to meet Him any day and share this gospel with others along the way.

Shield of Faith

The shield of faith protects the believer against injury, and it safeguards against the enemy. Faith must be continuous to be beneficial. Faith brings about confidence in our relationship with Christ. Faith empowers us to go beyond just knowing who God is and who we are in Him to acting on that knowledge and belief. According to Hebrews 1:11, "Faith shows the reality of what we hope for; it is the evidence of things we cannot see." Faith assures us that even when we cannot see or fathom something, God is still working and fulfilling promises, making ways, and moving on behalf of the believer. When a believer has faith, we wholly rely and depend on God to stay true to His Word. When faith and hope accompany love, we can surrender to God's guidance in obedience and we have peace and reassurance in the will of God. To handle the shield of faith effectively, the believer must trust in God completely, knowing that God will not lie or change His mind (1 Sam. 15:29, Heb. 6:8). "It is impossible to please God without faith. Anyone who wants to come to him must believe that God exists and that he rewards those who sincerely seek him" (Heb. 11:6).

Faith within the believer can grow over time with experience. Paul shares that "Abraham never wavered in believing God's promise. His faith grew stronger, and in this he brought glory to God. He was fully convinced that God is able to do whatever he promises" (Rom. 4:20–21). Experience is a teacher of the faith. As the believer practices believing and trusting God, they will see His faithfulness and, in turn, build upon their faith. A little can go a long way with God. Just as He blessed two fish and five loaves of bread to feed more than five thousand people, He can stretch a mustard seed of faith into miraculous works and deliverances.

The believer must realize that God wants us to trust him with every area of our lives, not only the spiritual parts, but also in our relationships, struggles, education, jobs, finances, dreams, and hobbies. The believer should know that faith in God is what is going to allow us to overcome and make it through. "That is why I am suffering as I am," Paul tells us, "Yet this is no cause for shame because I know whom I have believed and am convinced that he can guard what I have entrusted to Him until that day" (2 Tim. 1:12 NIV). Patient expectancy should follow faith in the promises of God. "We were given this hope when we were saved. If we already have something, we don't need to hope for it. But if we look forward to something we don't yet have, we must wait patiently and confidently" (Rom. 8:24–25). For the believer to gain new ground through faith and save others, they must share the gospel. "So, faith comes from hearing, that is, hearing the Good News about Christ" (Rom. 10:17).

Helmet of Salvation

The helmet of salvation reassures and protects us from the enemy's lies and attacks on the mind of the believer. Our confidence in the love and the sacrifice of God repels all the lies of the enemy. When the believer knows they belong to God, no matter their mistakes or failings, they can embrace forgiveness with a repentant and grateful heart. Understanding their new status as a child of God and a conqueror allows them to walk with the strength of God's Spirit and not bow to temptation and fear. The helmet of salvation is a vital part of the believer's every day, every-occasion attire because it allows the believer to address life from a sure foundation. The believer needs to continually check that the helmet sits properly and covers them wholly because the enemy is cunning and does not slack on his attacks. He is always slipping thoughts and opinions into the mind of the believer. If the ideas and feelings don't line up with the freedom that Christ has purchased or the purpose of God for the body, we should cast them down at God's feet and prohibit them from ruling over our minds, discussions, or actions. As it says in 2 Corinthians 10:5, "We destroy every proud obstacle that keeps people from knowing

God. We capture their rebellious thoughts and teach them to obey Christ."

The hope of salvation is not to be hoarded but spread abroad, bringing deliverance and change into other people's lives. The hope of salvation helps to sustain the believer in troubling times, knowing their expected end: one filled with life, peace, and the presence of God. The hope that comes from salvation changes the believer's attitude and also transforms their priorities and plans. Confidence in the promises of God allows the believer to endure the process as they move from glory to glory, knowing that the end comes with a great reward. In middle school, I began to take my walk with Christ more seriously. As I went from day to day with some victories, some failures, and some standstills, I wondered if I had done well enough. One part of my mind would say, "I am fine, I have Christ, nothing else matters," but another part would taunt me with my failings. I felt unsure of my final destination. I thank God that He sees us and knows what we need. I woke up bothered one night and went to sleep with my parents in their room. I fell off to sleep and dreamed about seeing the gates of heaven open up to me as I lay curled on the edge of the bed. When I woke up, I felt happy and reassured that heaven was my final destination. This dream reaffirmed in my spirit that I would see Christ in glory, no matter what life brought. God affirmed His Word through that dream and ministered hope to my soul. That dream was God straightening my helmet of salvation. He readjusted the straps so that they were snug, and now I can continue to hold to the hope of my salvation and let it carry me to the end, no matter what obstacles or situations the future holds. "'For I know the plans I have for you,' says the LORD. 'They are plans for good and not for disaster, to give you a future and a hope'" (Jer. 29:11).

Sword of the Spirit (Word of God)

The Word of God is an active, powerful catalyst for change. We can use the Word of God not only to ward off the enemy but also to bring about spiritual growth, which is why it is part of the armor of God. The armor of God protects and defends the believer. It also ministers to the believer, bringing about deliverance and maturity as the believer wears it. Jesus is the Word of Life (1 John 1:1), and He shares His Word to bring salvation, protection, healing, and the power to change to the believer. The Word functions dynamically in various ways. The Word is discerning and cleanses (Heb. 4:12; John 15:3; Ps. 119:9). The Word gives faith (Rom. 10:17). The Word is active and productive (Isa. 55:11). The Word of God brings deliverance (Matt. 8:16; Ps. 107:20). The Word of God is living and powerful, and when the believer trusts and utilizes it in their life, the Word brings about transformation, healing, enlightenment, strength, and guidance.

Summary

The armor of God offers the believer the reassurance and resources they need to combat wrong thoughts, temptation, bad situations, negative attitudes, and the other various attacks from the enemy. We should be aware of the enemy and his tactics (2 Cor. 2:11), but we cannot let thoughts about the enemy consume our lives. We have more pleasant things on which to meditate (Phil. 4:8). God saved the believer for more than just fending off Satan. He wants the believer to live as an overcomer, filled with joy and peace and focused on our relationship with Him. As believers, we can live in harmony with the people around us and embrace others while boldly proclaiming testimonies of salvation.

REGULATING OUR LIVES

Many variables contribute to our well-being that can become unstable and cause us to get off-track. When instability and frustrations occur, we should evaluate ourselves and our situation to determine what is causing the disruptions or hindrances in our lives. Just as a thermostat regulates the temperature in a space, we should prayerfully take a read of our situations and address those things that have become destructive or unproductive. Utilizing God's wisdom and guidance leads us to identify the source of our issues and enlightens us on the changes and growth that are needed. We may have to change our habits, thinking, environments, and relationships to gain the footing that we need to get back on the track living a full life in Christ. If we do not take the initiative to correct the issues, we may do harm or damage to our reputations, relationships, careers, and self-esteem, all due to imbalances in our mental, physical, and spiritual selves. Our relationships, emotions, and way of communicating stem from our being and should be monitored so that we can readily address situations when they present themselves. Our mind, the decision maker, receives information from our physical and spiritual selves and processes it, then chooses a course of action. When we align our decision-making up with the Word of God, we gain grounds of stability and find wisdom on how to address the problem areas of our life. Choosing to align our thinking and actions with anything other than godly standards makes us prone to instability and defeat in various areas. Acts 17:28 tells us, "For in Him we live and move and exist." We need to stop running away from what gives us life and receive God's Word, which supports, leads, and guides us into being productive and victorious in Christ.

Managing Relationships

God created humanity for a relationship, not just with Him, but with others as well. He created Eve as a companion to Adam so they could encourage and help each other. Relationships are lovely avenues of blessing and connection, and they call us to change and grow through each of our unique personalities and backgrounds. We must be wise in these interactions and consider which ones are beneficial or harmful. We can divide relationships into several dynamics, but these three are the simplest: *mutualism,* wherein both individuals benefit from the relationship and each does their part; *commensalism,* wherein one individual benefits from another without contributing, but their activities do not harm the other; and parasitism, wherein one person benefits while harming the other by taking more than the other can give. God uses mutual and commensal relationships to help the believer heal, grow, and mature, and He doesn't condone parasitic relationships, because they oppress and distract the believer. Some commensal relationships can seem parasitic when we are not putting in the time and effort for self-care so that we can receive what we need to sustain ourselves in those commensal relationships. No matter the level of intimacy or length of time shared, interactions with others can be influential and even life-changing. We must have the mindset of dealing with people with love and compassion no matter the kind of relationship.

Relationships have benefits. There is strength in numbers when people come together, joining efforts toward a common goal, where great things can happen. Even when we cannot lend physical help to someone in need, we can give spiritual guidance by interceding for one another in prayer and sharing encouragement. There are times that we can depend only on God, but that doesn't mean we should reject the help, love, support, and camaraderie that God offers through others. Psalm 118:8 advises that "it is better to take refuge in the Lord than to trust in people," but trusting in God does not exempt the believer from forming relationships in the Body of Christ. Scripture urges that we "think of ways to motivate one another to acts of love and good works. And let us not neglect our meeting together, as some people do, but encourage one another, especially now that the day of his return is drawing near" (Heb. 10:24–25). In the Body of Christ, relationships are more about giving than receiving. God chose to utilize the hands, feet, and mouth of humanity to do His will on this earth. The believer must embrace their role as a resource, with God as the Source. God uses the believer to minister to others, and when we do not yield to God's call for us, we neglect to walk in all that God has provided.

God called the believer to be a voice to our community. Believers are not to sit idly by while others suffer or wander in darkness. We should bring light to others and encourage them to get on the narrow path of righteous living and stay on it. Hebrews 3:13 instructs us, "You must warn each other every day, while it is still 'today,' so that none of you will be deceived by sin and hardened against God" (Heb. 3:13). Many things try to distract and deceive humanity, and we must shine a light by living and speaking the truth. When advising someone and encouraging them in their walk, we must act out of love, because people are far from perfect and need understanding and forgiveness. The first book of Peter 4:8 reminds us how unique and powerful love is: "Most important of all, continue to show deep love for each other, for love covers a multitude of sins." The believer must not go around ignorant of the hardships and setbacks of their fellow believers and the rest of humanity but be willing to acknowledge where someone is and encourage them to where God is calling them to be. Proverbs 27:23 advises us, "Know the state of your flocks, and put your heart into caring for your herds." After recognizing someone's situation, we have to take it a step further and show compassion and enduring faith. We are to stick with those whom God has placed in our lives to influence and make a positive difference. Faithfulness to the vision of God in each of our relationships is vital because dedication and consistency are what nurtures and reveals growth and change.

The Believer Should Have a Type

The Bible tells us that Solomon is one of the wisest men to walk the earth, yet he aligned himself with pagan worshippers and took advice from fools. He allowed those who had agendas contrary to the kingdom of God to influence his thoughts and choices. Rather than correct and encourage him in the things of God, his friends, spouses, and advisers encouraged his ungodly behavior and lust. As Proverbs tells us, "Walk with the wise and become wise; associate with fools and get in trouble" (13:20). Even though Solomon was wise and did great things initially for the kingdom of God and His people, he eventually caused discord in Israel and split the kingdom into two parts, Israel and Judah. The first book of Corinthians 15:33 tells us, "Don't be fooled by those who say such things, for 'bad company corrupts good character.'" Those in the enemy's camp, like Solomon's advisers, can create witty phrases and sound arguments to tempt the believer away from the principles and character of God. Seeking for pleasure, satisfaction, and acceptance through carnal and unrighteous means ultimately leads the believer to destruction.

God warns us about the negative influence that the world and the people who have not separated themselves from it can have on us. For example, 2 Corinthians 6:14–16a says thus:

> Don't team up with those who are unbelievers. How can righteousness be a partner with wickedness?

How can light live with darkness? What harmony can there be between Christ and the devil? How can a believer be a partner with an unbeliever? And what union can there be between God's temple and idols? For we are the temple of the living God.

God does love the world, but He also knows that not all the universe loves Him. Unbelievers are aligned with the enemy's camp. The enemy's mission of rebellion and destruction is either unknowingly or knowledgeably chosen by those who do not receive the love of Christ. The world's agenda runs contrary to God's, and we should not allow it to sway our stance in God's love, will, and peace. God leaves us on this earth after salvation so that we can influence it positively by sharing the gospel and bringing others into the kingdom of God. We should use caution in our interactions with unbelievers, make sure that they do not have a negative influence over our decision-making and actions. Unbelievers will encourage us to deal with situations as the world would, and in the majority of cases, they do not adhere to godly principles. Unbelievers and sometimes even immature or backslidden believers share advice or display behaviors that can lead others to astray. Whether in malice or ignorance, those in the world will try to make immoral things moral. We are to show love and compassion to all; however, it should be done with wisdom and within boundaries so that we are not led astray because we have allowed wicked ways to influence our thoughts and choices.

Managing Emotions and Desires

Emotions have a purpose. They help us read how we are handling a situation internally; however, how we are feeling does not give us a license to sin or display ungodly character. The enemy can pervert emotions into a stumbling block or weapons used to oppress the saint and validate their participation in unrighteous behavior. Galatians 5:24–25 calls us to nail to the cross our sinful nature that desires things that run contrary to God's will and character and instead be led by the Spirit of God. When emotions are high, a person is more prone to fall back to practices of the old nature to accomplish the desired outcome. During times of emotional distress, we need to be more aware of ourselves, allowing self-discipline and wisdom to take the reins and place the emotions that want to drive us to sin out of the car. It takes practice, but as believers, we can stop our feelings and desires from taking control and leading us into negative behavior. We can choose to be led by the words and character of God.

Galatians 5 lists emotions and actions that come from the Spirit of God and those that are from our sinful nature.

> When you follow the desires of your sinful nature, the results are very clear: sexual immorality, impurity, lustful pleasures, idolatry, sorcery, hostility, quarreling, jealousy, outbursts of anger, selfish ambition, dissension, division, envy, drunkenness,

wild parties, and other sins like these. Let me tell you again, as I have before, that anyone living that sort of life will not inherit the Kingdom of God. (Gal. 5:19–21)

Emotions regularly make themselves heard. The believer's job is to manage them, quieting those that feed into ungodly thoughts and voicing those that uplift spirits. The believer must be purposeful in their thinking and actions, uprooting corrupt ideas and manners in their lives and sowing godly ones in place of them. The flesh resists that which is good and craves that which is unrighteous, but the believer must discipline themselves to reject temptation and accept the things of God. Yes, God wants the believer to enjoy life and experience happiness and contentment, but to give in to every craving of the flesh is a harmful and reckless way to live. The believer can control their thoughts and actions, and they can start by monitoring their desires and emotions. To maintain that control, they should subject the flesh to the Spirit of God and allow God to lead.

There is danger in giving control to our emotions. Proverbs tells us that "a person without self-control is like a city with broken-down walls" (25:28). Without self-control, the feeling of worry, anxiety, lust, bitterness, anger, and dissatisfaction would fill our lives and paint our lives with constant chaos, confusion, and unrighteous acts. God did not intend for the whims that come with emotions, situations, and desires to rule the believer but gave us authority and power to rule them. He wants the believer stable and at peace, and that happens when the believer is disciplined and looks to God and His Word for guidance. The flesh would have us wallow in bitter feelings and unforgiveness, while God would have us forgive and walk with others in peace and harmony. The flesh would have us indulge in every pleasure our body craves, making us unhealthy and creating a miss of our affairs, while God wants us to enjoy the blessings of life in moderation. He puts our hands to work so that we can enjoy and appreciate the fruit of our labor. Emotions and fleshly desires may be loud at times; however, we should discipline ourselves to walk in godliness and integrity despite the yelling voices. Moreover, we must not look down on others who struggle, because we all have an area in which we can improve. Acknowledging and working on ourselves keep us humble so that we are competent in encouraging others to work through their struggles. Paul reminds us of this in Romans when he admonishes us, "Don't think you are better than you really are. Be honest in your evaluation of yourselves, measuring yourselves by the faith God has given us" (Rom. 12:3).

Monitoring Communication

We use verbal and nonverbal cues to connect with other individuals and relay ideas, feelings, or information when communicating. Communication can be tricky at times as we try to determine what is too much and what is too little. We can muddy the waters if we give too much information or emotion when communicating, making it difficult for the receiver to identify or understand the significant parts. If we provide too little information or feeling, we don't give the receiver enough to comprehend the message. Communicating can feel like pleasing Goldilocks at times. We have to determine what amount of verbal and nonverbal cues are "just right" so that the receiver can understand what we are trying to relay to them. Sometimes, emotion and personality affect delivery, but in the end, the communicator wants to be heard and understood. Communication can seem more difficult for some than others, but it does not change its importance among the believers.

Growing up in a large family as the second youngest child, I was used to being overlooked, and I learned to go with the flow of others early. I didn't notice how this affected my communication skills until I was in high school. While I was having a conversation with a group of girls in the class, I began to share a thought but stopped talking before I finished without even realizing it. The girls sat there looking at me, not saying anything, and so I asked them what was going on. They said they were waiting for me to finish what I was saying. I laughed inside because I had finished the thought in my head but not out loud. I conditioned myself to do this because I was used to other people taking the floor before I finished my thoughts. I repeated my thoughts and was surprised when the girls valued what I said. This incident taught me that people listen even when you do not think they are, so I needed to appreciate the thoughts and ideas that I share, just like those girls did that day.

We must be similarly aware of our words and thoughts and whether they please God. Content and delivery matter in our communication with others. God cares about what the believer says and thinks just as much as He cares about what they do. We do not please God with cutting remarks (Prov. 12:18), foul or abusive language (Eph. 4:29), slander and backbiting (James 4:11; Ps. 101:5), rumors (Prov. 13:3), mocking (Prov. 22:10), gossip (Prov. 16:28), or whispered insinuations (Prov. 26:20). God wants the believer's communication to be encouraging, uplifting, productive, and healing, not a discourse that brings strife, discontentment, quarreling, and hurt feelings. We should heed 1 Thessalonians 5:11, which tells us to "encourage each other and build each other up." Monitoring what we say is a discipline that benefits us. James 3 not only reveals the power of the tongue but also gives us insight into our souls: "If you are wise and understand God's ways, prove it by living an honorable life, doing good works with the humility that comes from wisdom. But if you are bitterly jealous and there is selfish ambition in your heart, don't cover up the truth with boasting and lying. For jealousy and selfishness are not God's kind of wisdom. Such things are earthly, unspiritual, and demonic" (James 3:13–14). What we communicate not only allows us to share our thoughts and feelings with others but also reveals the struggles and victories we have encountered. Negative communication cannot be excused as "telling it like it is." God calls for the believer to use tact and wisdom in their conversation and living. The believer should communicate knowing that they do not need to share everything they think. When we communicate negatively, we should not try to fool ourselves into believing that we were coming from the right place. These harmful communications are a reflection of something being off within ourselves, and we should take it to God so that He can deliver and heal us from it. Negative communication is not an accident but a symptom that tells us that something is off, and we need rest, deliverance, healing, or nourishment (physically or spiritually).

Managing Our Authority

We must stay aware and vigilantly address the issues in our lives. Many of us, at various times in our lives, have tried to hide the enemy's activity, thinking we did not have the authority or power to refuse him. We gave him free rein because it was the path of least resistance. At other times, we would provide him with control because we decided to walk in disobedience and rebellion. Whatever the reason may have been for allowing the enemy a stage in our lives, we always have the authority through Christ to say "No." I encourage those who have not done so in the past to start doing so now. We have to realize, as children of God, we have the authority to tell the devil "No" and mean it. We are to resist him and watch him flee. Let's encourage others to walk in the victory that Christ has won for us and that God freely gives by first walking in it ourselves. I have to continuously recommit myself to refusing the enemy any ground in my life. Authority is a gift we should cherish and consistently utilize. Life comes with battles that require us to take a stance in God and His will so that we can overcome the enemy. We should take our stand in the love and authority of God, realizing the impact it makes on others. Our position in God can influence our spouses, children, and others in our sphere of influence to take notice and walk in victory with us. We may not always succeed, but we can endeavor to win more than we lose by the grace of God.

Yielding to the searchlight of God's Word and presence is a weighty endeavor, but one well worth the time, effort, and dedication. The enemy would love for us to stay in the dark about our weaknesses, strongholds, and hang-ups. He would like for us to be too intimidated by his presence in our lives to kick him out, but the love of God should encourage us to seek His wisdom. The Word of God tells us about the devil's devices, and deception is one among many of his tricks, as well as temptation. Temptation leads saints out of the will of God and into works of the flesh. I am continually learning and understanding better how God faithfully and mercifully pulls away at the layers of wickedness in my soul. He reveals another level of patience, of forgiveness, of kindness just as soon as I believe I am on decent footing. Once I begin to feel comfortable with myself, God reveals something that I need to work on, whether it is a bad habit, sin, or mentality. He also shows things that He wants to develop in me. God's grace sustains me through each day, and I look to Him to help me gain ground from the enemy and keep that which I have already won. "Search me, O God, and know my heart; test me and know my anxious thoughts. Point out anything in me that offends you, and lead me along the path of everlasting life" (Ps. 139:23–24).

Summary

As humans, we are multifaceted, consisting of more than just the soul. We consist of the mind (soul), the spirit, and the flesh. The soul is the essence of our being, while the spirit and physical flesh are the influencers. We can have and maintain stability within ourselves with the help of Christ and His Word as our foundation. We can build ourselves on His name and through His strength. However, to keep it all together over time, we must be diligent in regulating and maintaining the various areas of our lives. When our conscience or others we can trust to hold us accountable reveal an issue we need to address, we must be vigilant about adjusting, changing, and repairing where needed. Relationships, emotions, and communication are some of the main areas that we should routinely assess. Studying the Word of God allows us to examine our lives and make sure they are being guided by the standards God has established. His Word instructs how to properly maintain a peaceful and God-pleasing lifestyle free of instability, chaos, and the enemy's influence. He does not want us to be negligent or deficient in any area of our lives. We should wisely and consciously handle our relationships, emotions, character, communication, and authority.

PART 3

Impediments to Health

OBSTACLES *to* HEALING: UNWHOLESOME MINDSETS

Receiving God's help and completely trusting in Him takes faith, discipline, and practice. Just as Jesus Christ had to mature in His earthly body to fulfill His purpose, the believer needs to grow in their spiritual selves so that they may achieve their purpose on earth. The believer gains not only strength and understanding but also enlightenment as they mature. We must allow God to renew our minds so that we do not view our lives and situations through cloudy, distorted vision. We must see them through clear, enlightened eyes instead.

The believer has various opportunities and outlets to fulfill their primary purpose, loving God with everything they are and pleasing Him by showing that same love to others. Careers, ministries, relationships, and accomplishments are all avenues given to us so that we can honor God's purpose through them. The enemy aims to destroy humanity, but he must settle for disrupting the believer's growth and relationships. He does this most directly by tricking the believer into fixating on something other than their purpose so that they spend their energy on trivial and harmful things. God wants the believer whole, healthy, and triumphant, but this requires a process. As we work with God, learning and developing in the present stage of our lives, all the other goals and character building will come with time. A teacher does not worry about teaching the ins and outs of geometry to kindergarteners but shows them how to recognize and create shapes. God has a developmental plan for each stage of the believer's journey, and He tailors it to their specific needs, purpose, and personality. So long as we allow the Spirit of God and His Word to lead us, we can stay focused and productive in what matters most at this current stage of life, finding peace, contentment, and joy while there.

We go through different stages in life, and each has its challenges and rewards. However, it is counterproductive to fixate on previous phases of successes and failures. Frustration can occur when we try to push too quickly through stages, not fully grasping and applying what God is teaching. We can cause ourselves avoidable grief by trying to chart our path and choosing to ignore God's. Let us learn patience and not let the drive to finish and accomplish dictate how much peace and enjoyment we can have in our lives. Lean on God's grace and wisdom and allow Him to guide us, giving us the tools, resources, and opportunities we need without having to give up peace and contentment. As believers, we must learn to live in the now. We must put our hands to what is before us and not add to or subtract from God's plan and will. Matthew 6:34

advises, "Don't worry about tomorrow, for tomorrow will bring its worries. Today's trouble is enough for today."

Learn by Example and Avoid Learning by Experience

We have been warned against various things since we were little, from "Don't touch the stove" to "Don't watch that kind of show." These warnings are to protect us, and they were shared mostly from a place of wisdom and experience. When someone shared these warnings or advice, they likely realized the validity of it through personal experience or observation. Likewise, the instructions and warnings in the Word of God come from an all-knowing Source. He reveals to us the cause and effect of the choices we make through His Word and the wisdom or experience of others. He warns and guides away from unnecessary trouble and educates and leads us toward a promising future, freeing us from corrupting and harmful habits. In the Old Testament, the Israelites were stubborn about learning from examples or experience. They walked in cycles of unrepentant, sinful behavior and were repeatedly warned and reprimanded by God, usually through war and captivity. Jeremiah shares God's frustration with Judah, who did not learn from Israel's unfaithfulness and allowed the devil to tempt them away from their relationship with God. They are carried again into bondage and destruction as a result:

She saw that I divorced faithless Israel because of her adultery. But that treacherous sister Judah had no fear, and now she, too, has left me and given herself to prostitution. Israel treated it all so lightly—she thought nothing of committing adultery by worshiping idols made of wood and stone. So now the land has been polluted. But despite all this, her faithless sister Judah has never sincerely returned to me. She has only pretended to be sorry. I, the Lord, have spoken! (Jer. 3:6–11)

We can see how the devil still deceives and lures the people of God into bondage like that today. By continually showing people living in bondage and making it look healthy and pleasing, it callouses the minds and hearts of the degradation and harm to which it leads. Distorted carnal views of sex, money, society, popularity, emotions, justice, and relationships displayed by the world can lead many believers astray into spiritual bondage when biblical warnings are ignored. If we would only handle the different aspects of our being and life with the wisdom and in the parameters that God set, we would save ourselves a lot of pain and disappointment. God's Word and the voices of the Body of Christ will warn us of the enemy's deceptiveness. Let us not be so self-confident that we discard these warnings, believing we are untouchable or beyond it all. Let us not walk into the same traps and mindsets of those we have seen drift away from God, thinking that our experience will be any different. God continuously provides us opportunities to change interactions and choose ethical practices. We have to willingly heed the warnings and commit ourselves to walk in wisdom and integrity if we want to continue to walk in wellness and victory.

Don't Discard the Truth for Zeal

Zeal is good. It drives us to accomplish goals. But zeal without knowledge is dangerous. Paul remarks on this point in Romans when he says, "I know what enthusiasm they have for God, but it is misdirected zeal. For they don't understand God's way of making people right with himself. Refusing to accept God's way, they cling to their own way of getting right with God by trying to keep the law" (Rom. 10:2–3). Someone can cause more harm than good when they rally behind something that simply sounds good without knowing its real purpose. Zeal without wisdom can quickly turn into self-righteousness, which distorts principles and disciplines into rules that bring no lasting transformation or spiritual growth. Apostasy was a common occurrence that Paul and some of the other ministers faced during their time. People would preach their doctrine and attach Jesus's or God's name to it. They led many people astray as a result. In 1 Timothy 4:1–5, Paul gives examples of rules that apostates added, which were not marrying or restriction on eating certain foods. The apostates placed these extra restrictions on believers so that they could feel holier or more righteous. The apostates manipulated the Word of God and added weight to the people that Jesus did not give them to bear, and those who do this "are hypocrites and liars, and their consciences are dead" (1 Tim. 4:2). The overly enthusiastic person neglects proper instruction from the Word of God because they allowed themselves to be driven by passion and not wisdom. They quickly crossed over from grace into works of the flesh. These works of the flesh brought unnecessary restrictions and bondage when God explicitly offers freedom.

We must also practice Christian discipline, which helps us to stay true to the love of God's calling, with wisdom—never zeal alone. Dedication in prayer and fasting is excellent. We pray continuously, making sure to participate in our lives actively. Praying about promotion is great, but prayer won't do much if you do not show up to work. Sharing your hopes and dreams with God does not negate the need for the believer to take action and responsibility in their own lives. Communication with God will bring about deliverance, insight, and grace to accomplish what is before us. And we are responsible for acting with not only enthusiasm but also wisdom.

Resisting and Standing in Integrity

We are fleeing from those things that call us to sin and seeking after the character and nature of God. Surrounding ourselves with people who aim to please God helps with accountability and faithfulness. God calls the believer to be a conqueror in every area of our lives. When we are ready to fight the fight of faith, we let the enemy know that we are designating every part of ourselves to honor God. Luke 10:27 encourages us, "Love the Lord your God with all your heart and with all your soul and with all your strength and with all your mind." The believer must stand firm against the urges of the flesh and not let it dictate our thoughts and pursuits, tempting us into sin.

The enemy should not be allowed to utilize any part of us, our thoughts, or our person. Scripture tells us, "Do not let any part of your body become an instrument of evil to serve sin. Instead, give yourselves completely to God, for you were dead, but now you have a new life. So use your whole body as an instrument to do what is right for the glory of God" (Rom. 6:13). The flesh or sinful nature of man opposes God and continuously raises its voice, making sure to be heard in the decision-making process, and we must refuse him the microphone and time to speak. We must remember Paul's proclamation in Romans 7:18, "And I know that nothing good lives in me, that is, in my sinful nature. I want to do what is right, but I can't." Because the same applies to us. The flesh will always call us to follow temptation and yield to our whims and desire and let them rule us. However, this is not a hopeless dynamic; God has empowered us with His Spirit so that we could resist our sinful nature and subdue the flesh. Formerly, we were chained to corrupted nature. Now our decision-making ability is free from its power. We have a choice. The believer must continually make decisions to walk in freedom and not regress into old habits, controlled by our whims and urges. We must break bad habits and establish godly ones to strengthen our defense against sin. Paul tells us, "Don't copy the behavior and customs of this world, but let God transform you into a new person by changing the way you think. Then you will learn to know God's will for you, which is good and pleasing and perfect" (Rom. 12:2). Study God's

Word daily so that the flesh cannot direct the decision-making process.

Changing habits and behaviors is hard, and God did not intend for us to do it alone. He knew that we do not have the strength within ourselves to correct ourselves alone; that was why He saved us and gave us His Holy Spirit. When believers look to God for grace and strength to accomplish righteous living, they are delivered and grow in various areas of their lives. Moses did not get to walk into the promised land himself, because he sinned and disobeyed God in his anger, hitting the rock instead of speaking to it (Exod. 17). The adults who journeyed out of Egypt died in the wilderness and never saw the promised land because they murmured and complained and walked in disbelief. The Israelite soldier Achan and his family did not get to enjoy the promise because he decided to keep the spoils (whether out of greed or fear) instead of destroying it all as instructed (Josh. 7). The enemy tries to disqualify the Body of Christ from the promise and their purpose by tempting us toward sin. We must silence the voices within us and resist the temptation to walk out in fear, distrust, anger, lust, or pride.

Joseph had grand dreams of being someone influential in the eyes of his people. They were dreams from God, who intended Joseph to help and influence God's people in a time of famine. Many years passed before Joseph's dreams were seen, and he was a trial-seasoned man when he began to walk in the vision God gave him. Joseph had many disappointing transitions in life. He went from the house of a loving father to being abandoned in a well, to slavery, and then to imprisonment. However, at the appointed time, Joseph ended up in a place of significant influence and riches. With each transition, he faced trials and opposition, but we see he kept his integrity and did not fall to temptation. Joseph did not allow his situation to give him an excuse to sin, only an opportunity to honor God. Joseph might have been confronted with the temptation to doubt, to sin, to give up, and to turn away from the character and promises of God with each disservice he experienced, but he held on to his integrity. The enemy tempted and oppressed Joseph again and again, but in the face of it all, he honored God through his actions, and God rewarded him. In slavery, he did not lose hope. Joseph worked with excellence until his master trusted him. He fled when adultery tempted him and was oppressed in prison unjustly. In prison, he still aided others and interpreted dreams to minister to those around him. Joseph's willingness to look beyond his situation to help another set him up with an introduction to the king. He did not allow the temptations of doubt, fear, lust, and bitterness to distract him from a life of integrity because of His love and faith in God. He did not let difficult situations stop him from working with excellence and having compassion for others' well-being. Even when he did not see his promise, He knew God was with Him, and He was called to a higher standard of living. He went through life with God, showing Satan and us what it means to be loyal, honorable, and faithful, and God rewarded Joseph greatly.

Idle Living

A lazy individual must be one of Satan's favorite types of people. They refuse to take responsibility for the stewardship of their lives and bring about their ruin by doing nothing. Spiritual and physical laziness can have drastic effects on the believer. When we put aside daily maintenance and upkeep of the soul, it shows itself through our fruit. Through our inaction, we allow weeds of impatience, discontent, fear, and disbelief to take precedence in our interactions. We halt our growth and permit the world's harsh and deteriorating nature to steal away our promise, joy, and peace, and it brings about destruction in our lives effortlessly. Inaction and procrastination become our worst enemy.

The enemy needs only to plant the seed in your mind that says you don't have to do anything that you don't want to. You may have heard the statement "I don't have to do anything but eat, sleep, and die." This attitude is one of pride, selfishness, and stupidity, whether or not we acknowledge it. This statement expresses a person's unwillingness to comply with someone else's wishes. In reality, this retort simplifies life in a way that brings about no wise solutions. God placed us on this earth for more than just self-gratification and good times. Our vices vary, but whatever they are, we should never stop laying them at God's feet and preventing them from dictating how we live our lives and how we communion with God. A situation can bear down on us and entice us to put God and His way aside in exchange for harmful habits or sins. We need to resist the temptations at these times and use the Word of God to stand our ground righteously. We need to find resolve, confidence, and hope in the promises and mandates of God.

An unattended garden that once produced a bountiful harvest can turn into a field of weeds. The same is true of our lives. Our once-fruitful and victorious life can turn into a vast field of ruin and unproductivity. We observe ruins through pictures or during a drive or walk through an abandoned area. We see nature reclaiming towns or buildings that are not maintained. The same goes for our spiritual life. When we are not diligent in our stewardship and do not nurture our relationship with God, we allow the old nature to creep in and reclaim parts of our lives that were once fruitful and prosperous. We stay healthy and productive through the guidance of the Holy Spirit and our dedication to God. Proverbs 24:30–34 depicts the mentality and actions of a lazy man and the results of his inaction:

> I walked by the field of a lazy person, the vineyard of one with no common sense. I saw that it was overgrown with nettles. It was covered with weeds, and its walls were broken down. Then, as I looked and thought about it, I learned this lesson: A little extra sleep, a little more slumber, a little folding of the hands to rest—then poverty will pounce on you like a bandit; scarcity will attack you like an armed robber.

The vineyard owner of Proverbs 24 did not take the time to cultivate his land, and it went to waste. We cannot allow ourselves to become like this man, unwilling to put forth effort in our own lives. We should stay motivated to be prosperous and productive in Christ. We should not give in to slothfulness and allow thorns or weeds to grow in our lives, sucking every drop of aspiration and expectation from us. Be cautious of seeds of idleness. We cannot let them fool us into thinking that they are practices in rest. We must stay the course before us, working toward the vision and purpose that God has given. When we need a refreshing, let us ask God for it. Our hearts are the ground in which all blessings and curses are sown. It is our job to monitor our heart and yield it to God for cleansing and weeding. Acknowledging that slothfulness is a path to destruction and taking responsibility for our growth by watering and planting good things keep us looking to and depending on God. When negative comments and filthy ideas plant themselves in our heart, we should refuse them residence and pull them out. It is also our job to receive the blessings and promises of God and make sure that they are watered and fertilized with prayer, faith, and the Word of God. Let us look to the Holy Spirit to be the living water that sustains us.

God did not promise that we would receive all His promises without commitment to His plans. God wants us to be good stewards, faithful workers, obedient children, and committed witnesses. A believer cannot be those things and idle too.

Ungodly Substitutions

We sometimes cling to habits and relationships because of comfort, fear, or complacency, allowing them to substitute intimacy with God. We look to these things for relief, fulfillment, and purpose, leaving no space for the Spirit of God to move in our lives. Jeremiah referred to this substitution as cracked cisterns in the life of the believer. He says, "For my people have done two evil things: They have abandoned me the fountain of living water. And they have dug for themselves cracked cisterns that can hold no water at all!" (Jer. 2:13). When a resource from God becomes our primary source, it becomes a cracked cistern because we have looked to that temporal resource to sustain us. Jobs, money, pleasure, children, spouses, organizations, obligations, and recognition are all resources in having an abundant life, but we can misuse them, making them the focus of our lives.

We begin to look at them as our source of happiness and fulfillment in our lives instead of the blessings that they are. We have lost focus. The wrong focus can cause us to grow disillusioned and try to use these resources to bring about a fulfilled life. Looking to these substitutions to sustain and fill us will result only in frustration, disappointment, and emptiness. God is the source of life and all its blessing, and we can find it only in Him. In ignorance or desperation, we ask the world to fill these cracked containers, only to be dissatisfied when we bring them to our lips to relieve the thirst of our souls and find them empty. When the believer thirsts after anything but God's presence, they are destined to become dehydrated. Worldly entanglements that keep the flesh engaged may placate and distract us, but they leave the soul yearning for substance and living water. Believers must look to the real Source to get fulfillment and nourishment. Everything else is knockoff that has no eternal value. Colossian 2:8 calls these substitutions for godly wisdom "empty philosophies and high-sounding nonsense." These thoughts may come from deep thought, but the source is either a fallible man or the cunning, deceptive powers of this world. Christ is the only source that can provide life and make us whole; no deep-sounding philosophy holds power to do that.

The world advertises new brands of cisterns or ways to fleshly enrichment every day. They resemble those home shopping networks and internet pop-up ads continuously trying to sell us something that will improve our lives and make them more comfortable, more stylish, or more pleasurable. When we buy into the hype, we deprive our souls of real nourishment in the quest to satisfy the flesh, only pacifying it momentarily. We leave our soul yearning for something more. God wants to fill His people and give them what they truly need. However, we come to Him not wanting to offer ourselves to Him but for our broken cisterns to be filled. We look to Him to put more money in our pockets, to make people treat us better, for a job promotion, for a new relationship, but we do not open up ourselves to be filled by Him. God wants to fill us and bring healing, change, and wholeness to the inner man so that we can deal with the challenges and situations of life with His empowerment.

Our thirst can become so ravenous that we hold those broken cisterns out to God, asking for a little relief, a small blessing. But God will pour His blessings into something that cannot hold His living water. He created us to receive His presence, not the things, hobbies, and positions of our lives. God wants His people to discard those broken cisterns and look to Him to fill every area of our lives through a relationship with Him. God is waiting for the believer to yearn to be full of His presence, not just His blessings and provision. And when we are ready, He tells us, "Those who drink the water I give will never be thirsty again. It becomes a fresh, bubbling spring within them, giving them eternal life" (John 4:14).

Managing Emotions and Desires

Emotions have a purpose. They help us understand how we are handling and processing a situation internally. These emotions are real; however, they do not give a license to sin or display ungodly character. The enemy can pervert feelings into a stumbling block or weapons used to oppress the saint and validate their participation in unrighteous behavior. Galatians 5:24–25 calls us to nail to the cross our sinful nature that runs contrary to God's will and be led by the Spirit of God. When emotions are high, a person is more prone to fall back to practices of the old nature following passions, desires, and anger, not considering how we should be trying to align ourselves with God. During emotionally high situations, the believer needs to be more aware of themselves, allowing self-discipline and wisdom to take the reins and placing the emotions that want to drive us to sin in the back seat. Believers will know if their response displeases God after they familiarize themselves with what pleases Him. It takes practice, but we can stop our emotions and desires from taking control. Instead, we can choose to be led by the Spirit of God.

Emotions make themselves heard. The believer's job is to manage them, quieting those that feed into ungodly thoughts and voicing those that uplift spirits. The believer must be purposeful in their thoughts and actions, and they must not give space for immoral ideas and manners to take root in their lives. The flesh resists that which is good and craves that which is sinful, but we must discipline ourselves to reject temptation and accept the things of God. God wants the believer to enjoy life and experience happiness and contentment, but to give in to every craving of the flesh is a harmful and reckless way to live. The believer can control their thoughts and actions, and they can start by monitoring their desires and emotions.

There is danger in giving control to our emotions. Proverbs tells us that "a person without self-control is like a city with broken-down walls" (25:28). The believer with no emotional wall would continuously be flooded with emotions of worry, anxiety, lust, bitterness, anger, and dissatisfaction and feel that they need to act on them. God did not intend for the whims of emotions, situations, and desires to manipulate and control the believer. God wants us at peace, and that happens when the believer remains disciplined in the ways and Word of God. Emotions and fleshly desires may be loud at times, but that does not mean that the believer should indulge in them.

Instead, believers should discipline themselves to walk in godliness and integrity despite the yelling voices.

Moreover, believers must not look down on others who struggle, because we all have an area in which we can improve. We should stay humble, encouraging others to work through their struggles while we acknowledge and work on our own. Paul reminds us of this in Romans when he warns, "Don't think you are better than you really are. Be honest in your evaluation of yourselves, measuring yourselves by the faith God has given us" (Rom. 12:3).

Summary

We must stay watchful of our mentality and thoughts, taking care that they align with the character and principles of God. During our walk with God, we will face a lot of trials and temptations, and if we are not aware and vigilant, the enemy will craftily build stumbling blocks and strongholds. The enemy will overwhelm us in times of weakness to steer us toward the broad path of destruction. The first book of Peter 5:8 reminds us to be sober and alert because the enemy continuously patrols and watches for an opportunity to introduce vices. We must not use the freedom that God's grace gives us to rationalize partaking in things that lead to sin. We are responsible for our spiritual, mental, emotional, and physical health. We should not allow ignorance, bad times, idleness, or emotionally intense moments to lay waste to the potential that God gives each of us. We must continue to look to God as our Source and allow Him to feed our souls, putting in the necessary work, time, and study. We should lay down all our substitutions for God's presence and provision and yield ourselves to being filled and guided by His Spirit.

OBSTACLES *to* HEALING: FESTERING WOUNDS

As individuals living in this imperfect world, we encounter imperfect people and difficult situations. We receive hurts and wounds, and we inflict them. Those who are considerate and compassionate inflict less pain on others; however, offenses are inevitable in this fallen world. We need to learn to deal with hurt and disappointment in a way that does not alienate our view of the present or future. We often have no control over the struggles that we face, such as genetic health issues, childhood circumstances, or criminal acts against us. However, the believer doesn't have to allow those things to cast a shadow over their lives. In 1 Peter 2:23, Paul reminds us of how Jesus dealt with insult and suffering from other people's mouths and hands. He did not plan for revenge or threaten those who chose to do Him harm. Instead, Paul placed them into God's just hands. He prayed for them (Luke 23:34). When we decide how to deal with others who have offended us, and whether we should take it to heart, we must remember that we, too, have caused offenses (Eccles. 7:21–22; Matt. 7:1–5).

People can live through many situations that give hate, bitterness, defeatism, and unforgiveness as consolation prizes for their suffering. The problem with these consolation prizes is that none of them bring healing or deliverance. Instead, they are emotional bacteria or parasites that cause wounds to inflame and fester. While it is healthy for injustices and pain to upset us, we cause ourselves unnecessary harm and discomfort when we hold on to this hurt and do not allow healing. It is hard to let go of something when we do not have that next thing already at hand. However, God is there, waiting patiently to provide the healing, answers, and comfort we need.

Festering happens when one doesn't take the time or is unable to cleanse and adequately treat a wound and the infection is allowed to set in and possibly spread. Our emotional bacteria are not satisfied with affecting one area of our lives; they want to spread as far and as fast as they can. Our hurt inevitably invades and taints everything. If we do not take care of these negative emotions, they will affect our thoughts, conversations, relationships, sleep, dreams, and desire to walk in purpose. These festering wounds want us to relive, cry, and rant over the past with no intention of moving forward. They prevent us from flourishing in the present and finding hope, purpose, and growth in our future.

Hatred

Hatred can be a very destructive emotion that can cloud one's decision-making and build stumbling blocks to peace and joy. Hate is more potent than disliking something or someone. It morphs into hostility and resentment. It leads one to hope for bad things to happen to others or to cause those things to happen. Satan plays records of "hate" on repeat in the thoughts of people, keeping them boiling on the inside with negativity. So long as the believer listens to this soundtrack, they struggle to walk effectively in the love of God. Love is the remedy to hate. "Hatred stirs up quarrels, but love makes up for all offenses" (Prov. 10:12). Hatred would have us only to see the negative and never hope for more. Love looks beyond the nature and actions of a person and recognizes their need for mercy and salvation. Love speaks and creates life, while hatred only causes death: death to peace, joy, relationships, growth, and fruitfulness. It's like weed killer; you can use it thinking that it will take care of the unwanted things in your life, only to find that it has killed everything around that it has touched. Love is vital to hold on to when hatred tries to place roots in our lives. Love is more than a feeling; it is a condition of the mind that calls for action even in the face of contrary emotions. It is a decision that produces works that move with the welfare of another in mind. Love is a life-giving, life-saving, life-preserving force that brings about deliverance and healing. One can go through the motions, but God looks at the heart of man, and He calls the believer to a higher standard than the world. A level of living that rises above hatred and endeavors to walk in love.

In our society, one can hate those who do them wrong or hate those who are different in some way. Hate can be their prerogative. But believers don't have the privilege to hate anyone; however, they do have the power to overcome those feelings of hate with forgiveness and love. Differences, history, and pain are not an allowance for hatred in the Body of Christ. They are struggles, mountains, and tests that we need to confront and overcome so that we can move beyond them and embrace more of our abundant life. God provides His grace and strength to overcome and move past hate. The enemy would like each of us to get bogged down in hatred, letting it drain away joy, peace, and fulfillment, clouding out all the blessings and purpose of God. See hate for what it is, a pathogen that seeks out wounds in which to fester. Give those wounds to God so that He may cleanse them, and they can properly heal. Do not let hatred darken your heart. Love overcomes hatred because we cannot hate when there is a consistent flow of forgiveness, patience, hope, longsuffering, and benefit of the doubt given to a person or situation. Hate the wrong, but don't discard the person (Rom. 12:19). The only thing that we are permitted to hate is evil. People do evil things, and we should hate the acts but show the love of God in wisdom being led by God to find out what is called of us in those situations. We should always put them in God's hands and trust Him to handle them in the way He deems fit, whether through punishment, discipline, salvation, or judgment. God says revenge is His work not ours. The believer is not responsible for exacting vengeance or retribution. Hate only dampens your soul. Hate is a strong emotion that can overtake us when we are in pain and hurt, but we must not allow it to fester and contaminate our attitude.

In Matthew 5:44, Jesus tells us, "Love your enemies, bless them that curse you, do good to them that hate you, and pray for them which despitefully use you, and persecute you." Why does He tell us this? Because He wants us to be like Him. Jesus, in the face of our rebellion, disrespect, and total disregard for Him, loved us, blessed us, did good to us, and prayed for us. Everyone will not receive salvation, but God still shows love to all, keeping the door open for those who do want to change. There will be those who will have a change of heart, repent of their evil deeds, and walk away from the enemy's camp, and some will not. As it says in Ecclesiastes, there is an appropriate time and manner to handle everything: "A time to tear and a time to mend. A time to be quiet and a time to speak. A time to love and a time to hate. A time for war and a time for peace" (3:7–8). However, do not allow your hurt emotions to decide what time it is. The believer goes through seasons of hurt and pain, but there is a time for healing too. We must allow our wounds to be cleansed so that the time for healing can come. There is a time for love and hate in the life of the believer, but we are forever called to hate evil (wrong) and show love toward others.

Bitterness

Disappointment can work as a blinder to the goodness and blessing of God in an individual's life. It narrows the believer's field of vision, focusing only on what is not and stopping them from celebrating what is. We all face disappointments. Some hit us harder than others. Bitterness sets in when we choose not to move on beyond our frustrations and commiserate all the details of our misfortune. We ponder on these things, refusing to enjoy the good in our lives. Bitterness is a poison that harms the believer and hinders them from walking in the character of God. Hebrews describes bitterness as poisonous roots that corrupt. It says, "Look after each other so that none of you fails to receive the grace of God. Watch out that no poisonous root of bitterness grows up to trouble you, corrupting many" (Heb. 12:15). The longer you hold on to resentment, the stronger its hold on you. It grows into your thought patterns, speech, and relationships, putting a distasteful and harmful seasoning on everything you do. When bitterness sets in, people notice, and our words and actions become unpleasant not only to others but also to ourselves. God encourages us to look out for one another so that we do not drink from the cup of bitterness. He not only warns us about the danger of bitterness but also shares the remedy, grace. His grace allows us to forgive ourselves. It empowers us to be gracious to others who have caused disappointment in our lives. Ephesians advises us, "Get rid of all bitterness, rage, anger, harsh words, and slander, as well as all types of evil behavior. Instead, be kind to each other, tenderhearted, forgiving one another, just as God through Christ has forgiven you" (Eph. 4:31–32).

Defeatism

A mentality of defeatism completely contradicts the principles and Word of God. There should be no presence of it in the believer. A believer should not resign themselves to failure. A person does not put forth their best effort when they leave themselves to disappointment and loss, and some do not even try. Yet Colossians tells us, "Work willingly at whatever you do, as though you were working for the Lord rather than for people" (3:23). Does God deserve less than the believer's best? Romans 8:28 tells us, "God causes everything to work together for the good of those who love God and are called according to his purpose for them." Through everything, God is working for the believer's well-being, and He expects the believer to put forth their best. We concentrate on success and failures and forget about our real purpose—relationship. Defeatism puts more emphasis on what we can accomplish within ourselves, rather than focusing on walking and communicating with God. We gain real success not solely in winning and achieving but in growing, understanding, and helping others to do the same in Christ. When the believer stops looking for the win and starts looking to God, the possibility of defeat does not faze them. Whatever happens works toward their betterment because they have accepted His will.

Don't run from obstacles back into bondage. After Israel witnessed all the miracles God had done for them and experienced His love and provision, the Israelites wanted to turn back because of daunting obstacles rather than receive the fullness of God's promises. They said, "Didn't we tell you this would happen while we were still in Egypt? We said, 'Leave us alone! Let us be slaves to the Egyptians. It's better to be a slave in Egypt than a corpse in the wilderness!'" (Exod. 14:12). The Israelites faced many obstacles, but God never left or forsook them. Yet they wanted to turn their backs on God and return to slavery to avoid hardships. They choose to live their lives in defeat each time they put aside honoring and depending on God. Let us not do the same. Let us put our total trust in God, knowing He will provide. We, as believers, should not settle with a life of bare minimum when He has offered us an abundant one, which includes the fulfillment of His promises and purpose for our lives.

Fear can set in when we confront daunting obstacles, but we, as believers, must not allow it to be a chain of bondage in our lives, keeping us from embracing all the things God has for us. Fear of disappointment or failure keeps us from trying something new or better. Fear prevents believers from believing in their success in accomplishing the vision that God has given. We must recognize that God does not give us these feelings or emotions, "for God has not given us a spirit of fear and timidity, but of power, love, and self-discipline" (2 Tim. 1:7). Fear can be used by the enemy to cripple the believer from moving forward. The believer should refuse what that devil hands out. God gave the believer power, love, and discipline to overcome and conquer their struggles so that they may fulfill their God-given purpose. God wants the believer to discuss goals with Him before pursuing new ones, taking the time to ask for wisdom and guidance. He also wants us to do the same after failures. I learned over time that failure is not useless;

it allows us to learn and refocus so that we may effectively address those things before us. Learn from failure and place your hope and faith in God's promises.

We should not discard the promises of God because giants oppose us. In Numbers 13, Moses sends out twelve scouts to explore Canaan, the land of milk and honey that God had promised them. The scouts explored the promised land for forty days, then reported back to Moses. They shared that the nation was as remarkable as God had promised, but they discouraged the Israelites from walking in their promise and conquering the enemy because there were giants present. These giants made ten of the scouts feel insignificant in their presence. The report of obstacles and giants struck fear in the people, and they rebelled. In the face of opposition, they dismissed the promises of God and called for new leadership. They wanted to return to Egypt. Joshua and Caleb were the only scouts that urged the people to take ahold of God's promise because their confidence was based on a faithful God and not on their strength. Because of the rebellion and refusal to walk in the things of God, the people wandered the wilderness for forty years, and the older adults never experienced the promised land. Joshua and Caleb, however, did get to see the promised land because of their trust and faith in God. We must not let the presence of obstacles and opposition cause us to rebel and accept less than what God has promised and provided for us. How big the opponent or obstacle does not entail a more significant failure but the extended amount of faith and trust we will need to place in God's will and promises.

Expecting failure causes the believer to turn away from faith in the promises, power, and love of God, and it places fear above one's faith. A coach is not able to make a boxer fight. A coach can provide knowledge and help the athlete develop skills and talents. If an athlete concedes defeat before the match begins, what can the coach do but look on? The believer cannot win until they are ready to fight. God's Word declares that the believer is more than a conqueror through Him, but defeatism oppresses the believer from getting up and trying again. God did not promise that we would succeed immediately in everything we do, but He did guarantee that He would be there with us in our defeats, failures, successes, and triumphs. He will be there with us to commiserate, heal, celebrate, rest, plan, and provide strength as we walk toward the next thing.

God Is Our Source of Triumph

He gives power to the weak and strength to the powerless. Even youths will become weak and tired, and young men will fall in exhaustion. But those who trust in the Lord will find new strength. They will soar high on wings like eagles. They will run and not grow weary. They will walk and not faint (Isa. 40:29–31).

We are more than overcomers and conquerors because He loves us. We are more than soldiers out to defeat the enemy; God loves us, and we are His children. In our daily battles, whether we win or lose, He sticks with us. God is not impatient about our failures and doesn't think less of us for our mistakes.

He wants success for us and will teach and develop within us the character and skills we need to be successful.

In the same way, I had a great math teacher whose teaching methods set the student up for success in her class. She wanted to get through the material, but she was mostly concerned with her students' success. After she graded tests, she allowed us to correct the problems we got wrong. It didn't matter if you had received 50 percent or 96 percent. You had another opportunity to fix what was wrong to receive 100 percent. She did not give us another set of problems or make us guess which ones were wrong. She returned the graded paper to us and let us correct our mistakes so that we could learn the formulas and readily apply them. She wanted everyone to do well, so she gave us multiple chances to accomplish that. God is also more concerned that we understand His principles well and can apply them correctly in our lives. He is more concerned that we gain understanding to live life righteously rather than the amount of time it takes for us to arrive at a solution. God does not tally our successes and compare them with others to determine valedictorians; He invests in each believer's success and doesn't want them caught in a cloud of expected failure, unwilling to try. God has a different scoring system than humanity. He knows that accomplishments follow maturity and growth.

Unforgiveness

Unforgiveness can plague a believer in two different ways—their ability to forgive others and their ability to receive forgiveness. God does not give mercy to those who are merciless. God called the believer to be like Him, forgiving those who ask for it: "If you forgive those who sin against you, your heavenly Father will forgive you. But if you refuse to forgive others, your Father will not forgive your sins" (Matt. 6:14–15). At times of pain, the flesh wants the believer to refuse forgiveness for the offense and concentrate on the pain or transgression. Grudges and offenses will cause a person to pick at their wounds, causing them to reopen and never truly heal. When we do not forgive, we refuse to be treated and cling to the pain instead of the cure. As believers, we relinquish the opportunity to hold grudges because we had agreed to forgive a person seven times seventy for each of their transgressions when we accepted God's grace. The believer needs to embrace the healing that forgiveness leads to and lay aside the self-righteousness and condemnation that unforgiveness offers.

Jesus did not join the crowd accusing the woman of adultery. According to John 8:10–11, "Jesus stood up again and said to the woman, 'Where are your accusers? Didn't even one of them condemn you?' 'No, Lord,' she said. And Jesus said, 'Neither do I. Go and sin no more.'" Jesus calmed the crowd and asked for self-reflection instead of punishment. God does not want payment when the believer sins. He already received it through the sacrifice of His Son. God wants repentance. Jesus wanted for the woman caught in adultery to receive the same thing that He wants for us—forgiveness. Jesus wants us to acknowledge the wrong that we have done and walk away from it. Jeremiah lets us know that God's mercy is new every morning, and He lets yesterday's sins remain with yesterday so that we can walk in the freedom of forgiveness today. Do not allow guilt to weigh you down when God offers you a present and future full of possibilities.

The Source of Festering

Fear makes us fester—fear that no one loves us, that no one cares about the trouble we go through. If someone truly cared, we would not have gone through that trouble or have been spared the experience. We fear that no one sees or witnesses our struggles. We fear that we are insignificant and that our experiences prove that we are unworthy of love or consideration. We fear that we will lose our sense of control, so we act out and do whatever we can to avoid experiencing that make us feel like no one cares. We memorialize our hurt as a testament to the pain we experienced and even the pain we caused others in hopes that the memorial will ward off future indiscretions. As mentioned earlier, fear does not come from God, so all the thoughts that go with it are false. Fear opposes the love, power, or character of God. The first book of John 4:18 tells us that God's love expels fear and that "such love has no fear because perfect love expels all fear. If we are afraid, it is for fear of punishment, and this shows that we have not fully experienced his perfect love." God loves us and sacrificed His Son for us. Jesus came to this earth to not only witness but also experienced the pains of humanity. In Matthew 9:36, we see Jesus's compassion for the sick, tired, and hurt people of this world. He did not want to leave them without help, so He told His disciples to pray to God to provide people to minister to those who are hurting. Jesus, in His fleshly body, was only one person and unable to touch so many lives at that time without the assistance of others. Now He sits on the right hand of God, empowering His Body through His Spirit to meet the needs of His people.

Jesus endured our deserved punishment not so we could feel guilty and nurse our wounds but so we could receive forgiveness, give forgiveness, and heal.

> Yet it was our weaknesses he carried; it was our sorrows that weighed him down. And we thought his troubles were a punishment from God, a punishment for his own sins! But he was pierced for our rebellion, crushed for our sins. He was beaten so we could be whole. He was whipped so we could be healed. (Isa. 53:4–5)

Jesus was without sin and went to the cross and bore the sins of humanity. Christ knows about wounds and pain. He was denied and left by those who had followed Him. He was slandered and beaten for things He did not do. He went through this so that He could understand our pain and struggles. He did it so that we could heal our wounds. The trials and struggles of man are due to the sin and evil that plague this world, and everyone has their situation and struggle to face; however, that does not mean God loves us any less. God is there to walk with us through it all, ensuring our victory if we allow Him to work through us during those times. Fear would have us to build an idol for our pain rather than look to God for our healing. God gives us power, love, and sound mind to overcome our wounds and hurts:

- The power that allows us to face our past and present situations without emotions deciding our course of action but the truths and provision of God
- Love that covers a multitude of faults and allows others to grow and learn from
- Sound mind that dispels the lies of fear and pain and grabs ahold of the healing and strength of God's Word and Spirit.

We can only control ourselves, so let's use that control to be productive and mature, taking responsibility for how we respond to our wounds and nurturing them toward healing instead of allowing infection and causing reinjury. We must denounce fear and move forward regardless of its presence. We must show the enemy that he cannot dictate how we handle our lives and choose to glorify God in every situation. Fear happens. It is natural, but it is a feeling like anger; you do not have to hold on to it. You can choose to let it go so that it will not lead you into sin and stagnation.

Christ showed us the proper way to deal with suffering and persecution:

For God called you to do good, even if it means suffering, just as Christ suffered for you. He is your example, and you must follow in his steps. He never sinned, nor ever deceived anyone. He did not retaliate when he was insulted, nor threaten revenge when he suffered. He left his case in the hands of God, who always judges fairly. (1 Pet. 2:21–23)

Jesus demonstrates that we can trust God to handle those people and situations that have caused us pain. We do not need to make plans for revenge or throw around threats; those things do not bring God glory, nor do they bring the believer any closer to healing or peace. We must learn to continually trust that God has our best interest at heart and will carry out justice on our behalf.

Believe God Sees, and He Cares

God sees us and our situation, and He cares. He wants to bring healing, peace, and deliverance to His people. We are not exempt from pain just because we are children of God: others will still mistreat, disrespect, abuse, and ignore us. God is the only one who will not misuse and abuse us. He does discipline and corrects those He loves, but it is to make us better, by growing and enlightening us. Even when we experience things that bring shame and confusion, God can heal and deliver us. "For your shame, ye shall have double; and for confusion they shall rejoice in their portion: therefore, in their land, they shall possess the double: everlasting joy shall be unto them"

(Isa. 61:7 KJV). In place of our shame and confusion, He gives us double. What is this double? It was manifested in Job's life after he suffered significant loss and poor health: "When Job prayed for his friends, the Lord restored his fortunes. The Lord gave Job twice as much as before!" (Job 42:10). God gives Job more children, doubles his finances, and doubles the servants. At the end of the trial, he also gains the joy of knowing God even more. Job received blessings after suffering in a way that honored God. He allowed himself to be taught and come out on the other side of his trail wiser. God blessed Job with more than just physical blessings at the end of the trail, but he built up Job, and His soul prospered.

Whether we want to accept it or not, God utilizes the good, the bad, as well as the ugly to transform us into the image of His Son. He does not waste an opportunity to empower, strengthen, educate, develop, or deliver us from the binds of our sinful nature. Many of us have reflected on our lives and tried to identify why we experienced terrible things, whether they were caused by our own choices or another's. Some of these are senseless, cruel, and painful, yet we have and can endure them and look to God to create something beautiful out of them (Isa. 61:1–3). We must also resist the urge to try to assist God with His job. When we work out our means for validation and justification, we stop trusting Him to handle His business and care for His child. We have to change our attitude from one of contempt to one of humility toward God. God did not forgive us because we deserved it. We should remind ourselves over and over that our bad attitudes, anger, and bitterness do not help us; they only hinder God's movement in our lives. When we refuse to walk in love and forgiveness, we block God from healing and blessing us as He would like.

Summary

Holding on to negative emotions about life's pains and hurts discourages the believer from walking in the healing that God provides. The hurts and strains of life help us to acknowledge that something is wrong and needs to be corrected, changed, or put away. The feelings of betrayal, loss, and disappointment try to immobilize us, stopping us from seeking and receiving the help, deliverance, support, and healing that we need. Those negative emotions can cause us to close ourselves off from the healing we need. Holding on to the pain causes festering of bitterness, defeatism, and unforgiveness. These emotions push us to walk away from the path of love and pursue vengeance or self-preservation. Healing is a process, and we must be patient, allowing God to cleanse us of those things that hinder our healing. As we yield to God's ministrations, we must also take responsibility for our part in the healing process, which is to let go of the things that reopen, reinjure, or infect our wounds. We must look to God, our caregiver, for guidance on handling life after hurt so that we walk toward healing rather than stand in misery.

DETERRENTS *to* HEALTH: DIET *and* NUTRITION

God has given us a broad selection of spices and seasonings to make food pleasing to eat, but the purpose of food is to provide the body with nutrients and sustenance so that our body may function, develop, and grow. The same applies to His Spirit and His Word; He has availed Himself and His wisdom to the Body of Christ so that they may eat of Christ and grow.

Jesus replied, "I tell you the truth, you want to be with me because I fed you, not because you understood the miraculous signs. But don't be so concerned about perishable things like food. Spend your energy seeking the eternal life that the Son of Man can give you. For God, the Father has given me the seal of his approval."

"For my flesh is true food, and my blood is true drink. Anyone who eats my flesh and drinks my blood remains in me, and I in him. I live because of the living Father who sent me; in the same way, anyone who feeds on me will live because of me. I am the true bread that came down from heaven. Anyone who eats this bread will not die as your ancestors did (even though they ate the manna) but will live forever." (John 6:26–27, 55–58)

As we mature in Christ, we should go beyond being amazed by what Jesus has, can, and will do for us and take it a step further and begin to understand why. Our relationship with Jesus is more than satisfying our physical needs and wants. Being connected to Jesus moves us beyond the physical and into relishing in the spiritual freedom and power that He has given us. We should not look only at the miraculous and the exciting things of God and think that they are all we need to experience a full and transformed life in Christ. Miracles and blessings are fantastic, but they are mainly seasoning and desserts of life. God's Spirit and Word are the water, meat, and bread that will bring about growth and development and the ability to walk a righteous, godly life. God does not mind blessing His people, but He concerns Himself more with our spiritual needs than our earthly wants. As believers, we must tame our desires for only the sweets of Christianity and also consume the life-sustaining water, bread, and meat of the Word.

With how our society talks about dieting, one would think a diet is something you do for an allotted amount of time to get healthy or to obtain a tangible result. However, diet simply means what you eat, whether healthy or unhealthy. As

Christians, we must decide what kind of lifestyle we want and then establish a diet that will support it. If we're going to be victorious, mature, productive members of the Body of Christ, we can diet accordingly, coupling a good variety of prayer, Bible study, mediation, witnessing, and faith, among others. Just as in the food pyramid, we need more servings from some categories than others; we as believers only grow and properly function, getting balanced nutrition.

Overindulging and Wastefulness

God's Word is good for the believer, but we must digest even His Word with wisdom so that it brings about the most benefit. When believers gorge on the Word of God but do not exercise their faith, they gain a wealth of knowledge but no meaningful growth. Satan knows the Word of God, but that knowledge does not make him righteous, godly, or part of the Body of Christ. The Word of God not only inspires and comforts the believer but also brings about wisdom, correction, and guidance, which aids in spiritual growth. Once we receive the Word of God, we still have to choose whether we do something with this knowledge.

Food is a source of energy that fuels the body so it can function. However, you gain weight if you eat without burning the calories you consume. Typically, when there are extra calories not utilized, they are stored as fat. In moderation, this is good, yet when we overeat fat is stored, we can gain weight and have various health issues. Some believers consume the Word of God, gaining knowledge only so that others see them as knowledgeable. They become puffed-up. They love to know, but they hesitate to apply and exercise those principles so that they can become more reliable and function properly within the body. They lack the fruit of faith, love, kindness, self-control; instead, they act self-righteously, judgmentally, and disapprovingly, judging the world around them rather than using it to improve it. Believers should put to use the knowledge they have gained, exercising those principles and truths of God, obtaining muscle and strength, empowering themselves to walk through the day triumphantly, positively influencing the world around them. It is unhealthy to carry around all that knowledge, using it to rationalize everything and everybody without actually exercising it. When one applies the Word of God with understanding and humility, they do not make a stumbling block of the Word of God.

Jesus scolded the crowd when they continued to ask for answers but never used them. They would come to Him asking for more solutions without applying the initial answers He gave them. They piled their plates with the Word and presence of God and then would not eat any of it. When a believer goes from service to service, conference to conference, prayer meeting to prayer meeting and does not take the time to consume what is served, they become disillusioned. They expect so much from the Word of God, relating to His promises and provision, but they do not see them in their lives. They ask for more, wanting to feel the power of the Word, but they never step out and use it. Believers can get stuck in a vicious cycle, always looking for what God can do for them but never doing what God has empowered them to do for themselves. Believers can lose faith because they decided collecting things on their plate would bring them the benefits they needed, without ever actually consuming and applying the Word. They treat the promises of God and His Word as trinkets to look at, not as actionable mandates, so instead of performing the truths of God, they admire them and think how nice it would be to see those things manifested in their lives. God's Word is there for all to receive, but it only benefits believers who utilize and exercise it.

Bring Something to the Table

When the body does not receive proper nutrients, it cannot function properly. The Body may survive and deal with insufficiencies, but not without decreasing the quality of life. When we do not allow the fruit of the Spirit to grow and develop in our lives, we lack the essentials that we need to function and live an abundant life. Spiritual nourishment is essential to producing righteous fruit: "The Holy Spirit produces this kind of fruit in our lives: love, joy, peace, patience, kindness, goodness, faithfulness, gentleness, and self-control" (Gal. 5:22–23). When we eat of the spiritual food that God provides and heed to the instruction God's Word gives, we are working with the Holy Spirit to produce the character of God in us. The godly character is seen in the lives of believers who are led by the Holy Spirit. The believer that chooses God's way of righteousness over emotions, desires, and temptations maintains fertile ground for the fruit to be produced.

Each believer can embody and produce the fruit of the Spirit because we house the Spirit of God within ourselves. The seed of each of these emotional and social disciplines—love, joy, peace, patience, kindness, goodness, faithfulness, gentleness, and self-control—can be found in the believer. If a believer does not display or practice every discipline on this list, that is fine. Growth is about acknowledging where and what we can be and working with God to begin to see those things displayed and embodied within ourselves. Recognizing the need for the fruit of the Spirit in our lives and desiring to produce them is a start in the right direction. However, we should never stop at wanting to in our growth-and-developmental journey. Our desire should be followed up with learning, practicing, and consistency so that we can have lasting transforming results.

Each of the Spirit's fruits makes the believer a more reliable and avid defender of the faith and servants in the kingdom of God. Displaying this fruit in our lives helps us to write those inspiring letters Paul describes in 2 Corinthians 3:2–5. Let our lives be letters that others read and hold in their hearts. We are reading people each day; let our lives speak words of love, hope, and faith, shining a light to help others see. When we live in this fashion, others can see abundant life and desire it for themselves. We write these inspiring letters by talking, living, and interacting with the world around us in the character of God. When the believer can continuously produce and show love, joy, peace, patience, kindness, goodness, faithfulness, gentleness, and self-control in the face of adversity, they speak revelation and hope to others.

When we walk in the fruit of the Spirit, it strengthens us to handle stressful situations and rebound with love and forgiveness. It equips us to walk in peace and joy during any circumstance. If we live malnourished, fruitless lives, we argue, blame, and criticize instead of showing love and patience when something goes wrong. If we have little kindness, gentleness, and goodness within us, we become selfish, critical, angry, and demanding. If we have no self-control, we fall into every temptation, every bout of guilt, offense, and whim the enemy sets up for us. The fruit of the Spirit equips the believer to handle life in a righteous manner, which gives God glory and gives no place to the devil. Now that we are aware of the authority, power, and tools that God has given us and the fierceness of the enemy that opposes us, we must do as we are called and fortify ourselves in God. Take a look at this scriptural instruction:

> In view of all this, make every effort to respond to God's promises. Supplement your faith with a generous provision of moral excellence, and moral excellence with knowledge, and knowledge with self-control, and self-control with patient endurance, and patient endurance with godliness, and godliness with brotherly affection, and brotherly affection with love for everyone. The more you grow like this, the more productive and useful you will be in your knowledge of our Lord Jesus Christ. But those who fail to develop in this way are shortsighted or blind,

forgetting that they have been cleansed from their old sins. (2 Pet. 1:3–8)

God gave us His divine nature so that we could overcome the corruption of this world. Each believer has a choice once saved—to take ahold of their ticket to heaven and live life in defeat and blindness or grab ahold of all the blessings God gives to the believer. Allow God's divine nature to grow within you and take root. He will create you to be an individual who walks this earth in the fullness of life, embracing the better one He has for you on this earth and rejecting a life of oppression and bondage. When the believer allows the divine nature of God to define and guide our lives, we bring forth the fruit of His Spirit to sustain and deliver us in every situation.

Love, Joy, and Peace

Love, joy, and peace preserve the character of the believer and help guide their behavior beyond emotion and circumstance. Believers must work to apply the fruit of love, joy, and peace into our lives. The first book of Corinthians 13 tells us what love truly is. Real love allows the believer to look beyond ourselves and handle difficult people and situations in righteous ways. Love embodies all the fruit of the Spirit; if one walks in love, many of the other fruits will flourish in the life of the believer. Love allows the believer to deal with the ugliness of life without being tainted and keeps us from falling into the traps of unforgiveness, pride, faithlessness, hate, and discouragement. Love is a way of life that enables the believer to positively influence the world around them without letting the darkness of the world change them. Love looks for the betterment and well-being of another. We can love like this effortlessly when we are secure in the love God has for us.

Joy comes from knowing who God is and knowing that we are His. We are told this in 1 Peter 1:8–9: "You love him even though you have never seen him. Though you do not see him now, you trust him; and you rejoice with glorious, inexpressible joy. The reward for trusting him will be the salvation of your souls." *Merriam-Webster* defines *joy* "as an emotion evoked by well-being, success, or good fortune or by the prospect of possessing what one desires: delight." Joy knows that our relationship with God is eternal. The promises He has for us are coming, so we embrace the present, grateful for the well-being, successes, and good fortune that He has afforded us. Life in Christ should delight us even in the face of hard times.

Moreover, Christ showed us the power of joy by enduring the cross. The epistle to the Hebrews proclaims that "because of the joy awaiting [Jesus], he endured the cross, disregarding its shame. Now he is seated in the place of honor beside God's throne" (Heb. 12:2). By knowing what awaits us, we have the strength to endure the test, trials, and hardships of this life. With joy, we go through knowing that the things we suffer will bring about growth and make us more like Christ. The Epistle of James advises, "Dear brothers and sisters when troubles of any kind come your way, consider it an opportunity for great joy. For you know that when your faith is tested, your endurance has a chance to grow" (James 1:2–3). We learn to value the trials we face, and it helps us to live in the assurance that God is working on our behalf, conforming things to our good, for our betterment, and leading us toward growth and well-being. We have joy because we trust in a living and loving God who never leaves us (Rom. 15:13). Trusting in God helps us not become discouraged or overwhelmed by this world. We are to hold on to our joy with the confidence of the character, love, and promises of God.

In addition to love and joy, God wants us to stay in His perfect peace, an all-encompassing calmness that we are unable to get from worldly means. The world's promises of success, gadgets, and fulfillment cannot even begin to imitate the peace that God gives those who abide in Him. Peace comes from trusting and fixing our minds on the things of God instead of the troubles of this world (Isa. 26:3; John 14:27). We can receive peace and remain in it when we handle our lives in a way that pleases God, not looking for vengeance, speaking evil, or telling lies about others. When we turn away from evil acts and concentrate on being kind to others, we can freely walk in the peace of God (1 Pet. 3:9–11; James 3:18). God's peace guards our hearts and minds until we can see the move of God for ourselves (Phil. 4:7). We can walk sure-footed and hold great peace in this life when we allow ourselves to be instructed and guided by God (Ps. 119:165).

Patience, Kindness, and Goodness

Patience, kindness, and goodness are the fruits of the Spirit that help the believer deal successfully with the weight, pressure, and ugliness of this world. They sustain the believer and help us to overcome the enemy with godly tactics. While we look to God to do His part, we must continue to do the works that God designated us to do. Patience is a mindset that allows us to enjoy life and be content. At the same time, we wait for God to establish and bring about the healing, deliverance, solutions, and opportunities in our lives. We can be patient because we know that God cares and is faithful. Psalm reminds us, "Wait patiently for the Lord. Be brave and courageous. Yes, wait patiently for the Lord" (27:14). We can hold on to hope because we know that God has a good plan for us. Patience is not just waiting and wondering but standing faithfully on what God has said, knowing that He is there for us.

The believer must be patient as they wait for God's timing, enduring and persevering in our situation and with others. As believers, we are here to shine a light and minister to others, and we should do it with patience: "Preach the Word of God. Be prepared, whether the time is favorable or not. Patiently correct, rebuke, and encourage your people with good teaching" (2 Tim. 4:2). When we begin to understand the purpose and importance of each person's role in the Body of Christ, we have more patience toward others (Prov. 14:29). Our impatience and our hurt feelings should not stop us from being gracious toward others. However, tolerance does not require the believer to endure harmful or sinful acts from others in the name of ministry. While being patient with others, we should acknowledge God and ask for wisdom about our timing and approach to different situations.

Kindness is having honest and compassionate interactions with others. It entails doing right by others, no matter who they are or what the circumstance. Kindness, like all the other fruits, does not have stipulation or requirements for when it is applied in our lives. The fruit of the Spirit is made for every season, situation, and purpose. We should continue to exemplify kindness and all the other fruits, no matter what the circumstance—being kind shows that we respect the love that God has for all His creation and honor the image of Him in each person. Our respect for the image of God in one another is not contingent on if other people are willing to give that same respect. Kindness empowers believers to go beyond our prejudices and delight ourselves in treating others as we would like. Kindness is not *quid pro quo*. The Good Samaritan lets us see how to show genuine compassion even to a world that might despise us. Those that need our kindness may not be able to offer us any back. Empowered by the love of God, we should still be moved with compassion to assist others in need.

Goodness is the exact opposite of evil, and *evil* means to be morally wrong. When we decide to do good, we shine a light in this ethically darkened world. The light not only shines so that the doer can be seen but also enables those around them to glimpse God in their darkness. When the believer shines this light by doing good deeds, God is glorified and others can see Him in these acts and praise Him (Matt. 5:15–16). Right actions oppose evil and prevent evil from taking root. Romans advises us, "Don't let evil conquer you, but conquer evil by doing good" (12:21). Goodness enables the believer to combat the darkness of evil in their lives and the lives of others. As it says in Galatians, "Whenever we have the opportunity, we should do good to everyone—especially to those in the family of faith" (6:10).

The fruit of the Spirit are the attributes of God, and by bearing this fruit, the believer becomes more like Christ. Jesus wants to guide us to a place where we shine the light that reveals God's love by rooting ourselves in God and nurturing others. We can only be that light when we live as we are supposed to and do good works so that evil cannot have a place. When we are faithful to God, it becomes easier to comprehend what goodness truly is. The world's thoughts on kindness may have us believe that it is being kind and showing common courtesy; however, goodness is more than that. It is a loyalty to the right choices and morally good actions despite inconvenience to oneself. The believer should seek true wisdom so that we can effectively shine, bringing God glory to wherever we are and, thereby, combating the evil that is present. There are security and protection in wisdom, and there is wisdom in doing good. Proverbs is a book filled with knowledge and understanding and has this to say about its benefits:

> Then you will understand what is right, just, and fair, and you will find the right way to go. For wisdom will enter your heart, and knowledge will fill you with joy. Wise choices will watch over you. Understanding will keep you safe. Wisdom will save you from evil people, from those whose words are twisted. (Prov. 2:9–12)

Faithfulness, Gentleness, and Self-Control

Faithfulness, gentleness, and self-control are the fruits of the Spirit that help to sustain the believer as we walk this Christian journey with God. Faithfulness is an attribute that allows us to be consistent, loyal, and dependable. When a believer can walk consistently, devoted to doing that which is good, we are on track to flourishing. When the believer walks faithfully, they give no place for the enemy to triumph in their lives. In Acts 16, Paul and Silas were beaten and thrown into prison for their loyalty. Their imprisonment didn't look like a win, but it was because they remained faithful through their persecution and imprisonment. A jailer and his family received salvation because of Paul's and Silas's faithfulness. When we dedicate ourselves to performing the Word of God and embodying His love moment by moment, the enemy will attack. However, we should and can remain constant, like Paul and Silas, honoring God and shining the light for others. By staying faithful, we allow our circumstances, testimonies, and tools to further the gospel and love of God. Our faithfulness comes from knowing the love and loyalty of God. Our need for growth should not have us doubt God's faithfulness or His ability to ingrain increasing levels of devotion and dependability in us. We should not allow the instability, wavering, and hardness of the world to change us but instead highlight God's faithfulness and fortify our devotion in good times and during hardships.

Gentleness does not mean being someone's doormat. We should not allow others to sin against us unchecked or sin within our organizations or homes when it is within our right to disallow it. Leviticus 19:17–18 tells us to confront others in their wrong so that we will not be guilty of sin and can move beyond feelings of hatred toward love. Gentleness helps us deal with the situation in a loving manner by giving the care and consideration that we would want from others. We should not hate, dislike, or trespass against others. We should not look for ways to mistreat them or hope for their downfall. We are to love those around us, caring, understanding, and forgiving them as we would desire from them in return. When we are gentle, we are considerate and take measures not to hurt or cause trouble for others (Phil. 4:5). Paul tells us in Colossians 4:5–6, "Live wisely among those who are not believers, and make the most of every opportunity. Let your conversation be gracious and attractive so that you will have the right response for everyone." Gentleness is a practiced attribute, not an emotion that automatically arises at the appropriate time. As believers, we have to train ourselves to have the proper godly response. Just as you have to teach a child to pet an animal softly and without too much vigor, we have to train ourselves to handle the people around us with a gentle touch. Unbelievers listen to our words and view our actions, and they make inferences about the God we serve by the fruit we portray. Let us give them an accurate depiction of our loving and merciful God through our gentleness. He is not unmerciful and hardened, waiting to judge and punish them. He is a gracious God wanting to forgive and bless them.

The fruit of self-control guards us against the enemy, who seeks to steal everything we cherish. The second book of John warns us, "Watch out that you do not lose what we have worked so hard to achieve. Be diligent so that you receive your full reward" (1:8). The enemy uses strong emotions, like anger, disappointment, and curiosity, to tempt us to open the doors that will pour in chaos and oppression. Proverbs tells us, "A person without self-control is like a city with broken-down walls" (25:28). We should not let the enemy slip behind our walls and cause us to act without discretion.

Not controlling our thoughts, actions, and words, we put our relationships, careers, reputation, bodies, and peace of mind in jeopardy. Don't allow a moment, a circumstance, or a conversation to distract you from the order and wisdom God has given. We should not live our lives timidly or fearfully but wisely use self-control so that the enemy does not get a foothold in our lives. God wants us to walk boldly, but we can only do that when we are sure of ourselves in Him and we can fortify that assurance with self-control. When we are inconsistent about our stance and commitment, we give place to confusion and disappointment. When we do not embrace the principles and powers of self-control, we relinquish that power to our circumstances, our emotions, and other people. However, as believers, we do not have to live that way. God's Spirit has implanted that seed of self-control within each of us. Ultimately, self-control allows us to face disappointment, confrontation, temptation, and hardship. It will enable us to maintain the character and promises of God. Job said, "I made a covenant with my eyes not to look with lust at a young woman" (Job 31:1). We also need to make a covenant with ourselves and God to aspire to live a life of discipline, acknowledging those things that may entice us to walk out of God's character and staying watchful to avoid them. Commit to growing the fruit of self-control so that you can keep your blessings, purposes, and integrity intact. "Don't get sidetracked; keep your feet from following evil" (Prov. 4:27). If there is an issue with impulse control, professional help may be needed so that we can identify therapies, treatments, or constructive counseling to address those issues in our lives.

Sustained Fruit

"But blessed are those who trust in the Lord and have made the Lord their hope and confidence. They are like trees planted along a riverbank, with roots that reach deep into the water. Such trees are not bothered by the heat or worried by long months of drought. Their leaves stay green, and they never stop producing fruit" (Jer. 17:7–8).

Placing our trust in God allows us to establish ourselves in Him like that tree along a riverbank. Trusting in anything else will leave us barren. We will lack what we need to function righteously and handle our mental, spiritual, emotional, and social life. When we abide in God, we tap into the source of living water, which will sustain us during good times and bad. He will empower us to bear fruit in times of trial and struggle. To maintain and produce good fruit in our lives, we must continue to accept the Spirit's guidance so that He can nurture our development in these areas. We need to be watchful of our interactions and prevent the flesh from dictating our mindset or our responses. We must actively choose to emulate the character of God.

Summary

Studying and applying the Word of God help us to stay healthy. We need to exercise His principles and promises in our lives daily. We receive sustenance not only from God's Word but also His Spirit. God blessed us with an unlimited supply of fruit and water housed within ourselves through the presence of His Spirit. The fruit of the Spirit is the essence of God's character, which equips us to handle life with its blessings and challenges. This fruit flourishes in a relationship with God. God wants each person in the Body of Christ to be well-nourished and fruitful so that our needs can be met and we have enough to help meet the needs of others. When we are collectively fruitful, no one lacks and we can continuously grow as the Body of Christ.

DETERRENTS *to* HEALTH: NATURE *vs.* NURTURE

Nature

There are studies on nature versus nurture that try to determine how they factor into the attributes and mentality of an individual. Does one have more of a noticeable impact on our lives? Does nature (that given at conception) or nurture (our experiences after birth) determine who we will be and how we will interact with the world around us? I will say neither determines who we are, but they both greatly influence our choices, mentalities, and proclivities. The discussion of nature versus nurture is relevant not only to science but also to our individual lives as believers. Each day we are faced with a choice of which nature we will embrace, the old or new, and which one we will nurture through our thinking and lifestyle. After the fall of Adam, humanity became predisposed to sin, the old nature, but it did not take away our freedom to choose.

Humanity is now more inclined to pursue the lust of the flesh; however, we still can refuse to partake in ungodly acts or thoughts. Adam's disobedience opened humanity's eyes to all the evil possible and made us more prone to sin, but it does not dictate that we have to sin. Despite the sin that surrounded Noah, he chose to stay a good man and honor God. The ability to sin was not created when Adam and Eve rebelled; it only exposed us to the knowledge of it. Sin nature entices humanity to rebel against God and partakes in the vastness ungodly acts revealed. We cannot blame God for our evil desires or lay at His feet the depraved state of our affairs, because our immoral lust is ours and ours alone. The choice to sin causes the continued depravity we see (James 1:13). Humanity's willingness to sin against God and humanity is what creates a world filled with injustice, pain, and evil. All humankind has sinful nature; however, once we receive salvation, God's divine nature empowers us to walk righteously. Our choices are still ours alone. We have the responsibility of yielding to the works of God and nurturing the goodness He has placed in us through His Spirit. However, the presence of His Spirit still does not take away our free will. We can decide to nurture our sinful nature or be guided by the Spirit of God. As a believer, these natures war inside of us: sin nature versus God's divine nature. In each instance, we must choose which mentality we will allow to guide our thoughts and actions.

Some people want to blame their upbringing and the evil influences of others as a blanket reason for not doing better, for not trying. The things of our past color how we view and handle our lives, but once we hear the truth, it is our responsibility to make better choices. God will not hold our sin against our parents or any other individual, and He will not charge our parents' sin or another individual's sin against us. God will hold each person accountable for the choices they have made (Ezek. 18:20). Christ's salvation is not a conditional situation where the believer converts to a sinner with every misstep they make. The believer is reborn, and God no longer considers their past actions. We, as believers, have to learn to cast away our past and not allow it to affect our choices anymore. As Paul tells us, "This means that anyone who belongs to Christ has become a new person. The old life is gone; a new life has begun!" (2 Cor. 5:17). We must handle our inclinations and sins with the wisdom and grace God offers. Jesus introduced a cut-it-off, gouge-it-out philosophy when it came to the temptation of sin. In Matthew 18:7–9, Jesus acknowledges that attraction to ungodly things is inevitable and should be handled not with kitten gloves, but with a blade and a trash can. He instructs us to remove from our lives those things that would draw us into sin. Living an abundant life now and experiencing eternal life is far better than pacifying the cravings of the flesh. Jesus wasn't promoting self-mutilation or self-harm with his imagery of cutting off a hand or feet that would bring us to sin. Instead, he was emphasizing the importance of self-control and discipline when avoiding sin and handling temptation. The temptation is there, and it will entice the believer, but we must use wisdom, self-control, and needed separation to avoid the enemy's traps that lead to sin.

Nurture

We have a choice about which nature we follow and which we choose to nurture and give a place of prominence in our lives. As believers, we must not walk in denial about the lures of the old nature and be wise in how we fashion our lives so that we do not nurture the old nature and neglect the new. We all have things that tempt us and must acknowledge them and handle them with wisdom. We have to refuse those things that tempt us and not allow the old nature to dictate our lives. We must establish habits that help us avoid and resist the lure of ungodliness. However, controlling our urges is more than avoiding what tempts us. We must also introduce wise and healthy substitutions in its place that will sustain us when the desire comes. Breaking habits and addictions is hard because our past has trained us to follow the path to appeasing the lust of our flesh.

> Do not let sin control the way you live; do not give in to sinful desires. Do not let any part of your body become an instrument of evil to serve sin. Instead, give yourselves completely to God, for you were dead, but now you have new life. Use your whole body as an instrument to do what is right for the glory of God. Sin is no longer your master, for you no longer live under the requirements of the law. Instead, you live under the freedom of God's grace. (Rom. 6:12–14)

We must choose daily to stop our lust from dictating our lives and walk righteously instead. As we build habits to keep our unrighteous desires at bay, the cries for the bad will become weaker, and the voice of righteousness clearer. We must realize God did not intend for us to overcome our faults and sins alone. He provides more than just wisdom to instruct us but grace to empower us. Grace is more than God's unearned favor. It is His act of love of empowering us with the desire and aptitude to do His will. Paul shares that all the fantastic things he did for the kingdom of God did not exempt him for needing the grace of God to deal with his temptations and struggles:

> But I refrain, so no one will think more of me than is warranted by what I do or say, or because of these surpassingly great revelations. Therefore, in order to keep me from becoming conceited, I was given a thorn in my flesh, a messenger of Satan, to torment me. Three times I pleaded with the Lord to take it away from me. But he said to me, "My grace is sufficient for you, for my power is made perfect in weakness." Therefore I will boast all the more gladly about my weaknesses, so that Christ's power may rest on me. That is why, for Christ's sake, I delight in weaknesses, in insults, in hardships, in persecutions, in difficulties. For when I am weak, then I am strong. (2 Cor. 12:6b–10)

The believer must learn to lean on God and look to Him for strength. By the grace of God, Paul dealt with his thorn in the flesh so that he would not be defeated or hindered by it. He acknowledged where he needed deliverance and asked God. God answered not by miraculously delivering him but instead by giving Paul the strength to endure the thorn. God gave us self-control and discipline to train our bodies, and He has given us His Spirit to empower our minds and fortify His will in us. Establishing good habits and allowing God to renew our minds is something the believer will continually have to do to stay free from the grips of sin. Many times, we do not know how we will genuinely respond to a situation or temptation until we do. As Christians, we must lean on God's grace, which empowers us to deal with those surprise pricks and embedded thrones. The book of Jeremiah reminds us that we are sometimes unaware of what is in our hearts. It says, "The human heart is the most deceitful of all things, and desperately wicked. Who really knows how bad it is?" (Jer. 17:9). We may not always know our real motivation or where our choices will lead, but God does. Paul understood he could not handle his issues alone but needed God's grace to deal with those things that God chose not to move. He received a revelation about his problems; they did not define him but prompted him to find strength in God to endure and overcome.

Confront our issues. Dealing with sin and character flaws is a significant part of living life on this fallen earth, but they do not have to consume the believer. We will have to deal with them, but they do not have to overshadow our lives. We walk in the light and the freedom and strength that it offers. We can avoid the shadows of this world and walk with spiritual integrity in the face of temptation. When we do find ourselves in dark places of disobedience and rebellion, we are to repent and step back into the light. God is there, ready to forgive, restore, and encourage us to remain in the light. God does not want us in darkness, and the Word of God teaches us a way to handle sin and those who strayed. When we sin, we need to acknowledge it (Luke 17:3), confess and forsake it (Prov. 28:13), and then consecrate ourselves to holy practices (Rom. 6:12–13). When we are assisting others who have strayed, we are to confront the issue (1 Tim. 5:20), help them with wise instruction (Gal. 6:1), support them as they work to change bad habits (Gal. 6:2), and build them up as they try to walk the straight and narrow path (1 Pet. 2:2). Maintaining wellness is an endeavor that is dependent on the individual's dedication to spiritual, mental, and emotional hygiene. Some of the first practices in health that we learn are washing our hands and potty training. We learn early the proper way and place to rid ourselves of "mess." God instructs us in His Word how we should view and handle our messes and the messes of others, and by mess I mean sin, faults, and shortcomings.

The hygiene practices that we develop as Christians are for our betterment. Once we know better ways to handle life situations, we should use them. As it says in the Epistle of James, "Remember, it is sin to know what you ought to do and then not do it" (4:17). We may want to fall back into old habits, but we will be uncomfortable living our past life when we know a better way. God calls believers to a higher level of responsibility and accountability. We all have issues within our character and mentality that we need to address. Consulting God is important in dealing with these issues properly. He is merciful and reveals to us those old BC (Before Christ) ways that need to be addressed and instructs us how to do better. When we know better, God expects us to do better. The standard to which we are held does not change because of circumstances or people. God loves those around us and will reveal to them their issues when He sees fit. We should not allow other people's stages of growth to hinder ours. When God reveals a problem that we need to address, He instructs us on how to handle the issue righteously. He even gives us "refresher courses" when required. Let us be mature saints, and when God opens our eyes to the mess or issue, let us do as Isaiah 1:16 tells us, "Wash and make yourselves clean. Take your evil deeds out of my sight; stop doing wrong."

A tempered response to sin. We need to not only take responsibility for confronting our issues as we mature but also to mitigate our response to our failures and struggles. There should be some regret for our wrongdoing, but not fear of sin to the extent we do not enjoy the blessings that God gives us. As humans in this fallen world, we will mess up at various points during our lives—and that's okay; that's why God provides us with His grace and renewed mercies every morning. Our response to sin should not be skewed by fear or any other negative emotions. We should proceed cautiously, not fearfully, to avoid making mistakes and being lured into choosing sin. Holding ourselves accountable for our actions encourages us to walk a path that leads away from sin. The extent to the ugliness that humanity can participate in can be scary, but God did not give us the spirit of fear. He gave us His Spirit of love, power, and self-control. The believer should acknowledge the ugliness of sin, but we should not live in fear of what we may do or the potential of the ugliness in others. If we make a mess of a situation, it should not cause us to run and hide. We should look to God to cleanse and strengthen us with wisdom and self-discipline so that we can handle our lives better. When it comes to the ugliness of others, we must walk in wisdom and find peace in the love and faithfulness of God.

There is also another extreme opposite of fear, and that is confidence in sin, wherein we celebrate and walk boldly in our sins, daring others to correct or challenge our choices. Rebellion and disobedience become an accomplishment and no longer something that we regret. We work to obtain our fleshly desires with no regard to God or others and feel it is something that others should commend and praise. Unbelievers and some immature saints can be this way, wanting people to revel in their ability to sin and wonder why others don't join in their excitement. Not valuing our relationship with God or the need for correction is a sign that we are in a drastic need for a heart cleansing. God will not let those He loves to go without correction and stay in darkness. He will get His wayward child in line. As children of God, we should not revel in the pride and shame of sin but refuse to remain there and repent. God's grace toward us is not permission to sin but a life jacket that pulls us out of the messes we placed ourselves in and an opportunity to get back on the righteous narrow path. There should not be a callous attitude toward discipline or our indiscretions.

Seeing the wisdom in boundaries and standards allows us to have a tempered response to sin. Our enlightened moral compass and our relationship with God give us the confidence to experience the fullness of life despite the ugliness of sin in this world and the forethought to stay away from boldly walking into reaping the consequences of it. God knows who He saves, and nothing we have done or will do comes as a surprise or shock to Him. We should not deal with our sins, faults, and shortcomings according to society, our upbringing, or our rationalization. Immorality should be handled only how the Word of God instructs, which is to confess, repent, and move forward, walking on the narrow righteous path. Praying for the proper attitude to deal with messy situations and sin in our lives is wise. We have to work with God to cleanse ourselves from our wrong thinking, habits, influences, and actions to stay healthy. The choices we make about our companions, our speech, and our actions dictate how healthy we remain as we journey through this life.

Dealing with Guilt

If we continue to feel guilt or condemnation after God has forgiven us, we should remember that these feelings are tricks of the enemy. They are used to keep us from experiencing the fullness of God's love and grace. God uses conviction to get our attention when something is wrong or needs to be corrected. God wants us to recognize our wrong and then fix our behavior. We ask for forgiveness and then receive that forgiveness. After we acknowledge our wrongs, we avoid walking that way again. Guilt and condemnation are not parts of God's plan of reconciliation, deliverance, or healing. God told us, when He forgives, He forgets. He doesn't hold on to the knowledge of the transgression so that He can remind us later and make us feel awful about our past later. God cares more about our growth than holding our sins over our heads. He wants to move forward from our past so that we can continue to progress from glory to glory. Our fixation on guilt and shame only darkens our outlook and hinders our growth. God's forgiveness washes away the filth of sin. He teaches us through His Word how to make progress and grow in our relationship with Him. "But if we confess our sins to him, he is faithful and just to forgive us our sins and to cleanse us from all wickedness" (1 John 1:9).

Conviction without the acceptance of forgiveness morphs into condemnation. Refusing to walk in forgiveness leads us down a destructive process rather than a healing one. Romans 8:1 tells us, "There is no condemnation" (Rom. 8:1). Instead, condemnation is disapproval and punishment, and God said He does not have that for the believer. The believer can disapprove and punish themselves and other believers, but God does not. He doesn't approve of that behavior. As far as God is concerned, we became good when we received the works of Christ on the cross. We are now His children, and He takes offense when someone disapproves of His child, even when we do it ourselves. Conviction shows us that we are on the wrong track and need to ask for forgiveness so we can walk the correct way. Condemnation tries to immortalize our sin and hangs it about our necks as a weight to drag us down.

The enemy will chant in our ears our wrongs and worthlessness. His words try to drive us toward condemnation. He wants us to condemn and disapprove of ourselves so that we get lost, focusing on our mistakes instead of allowing God to cleanse us and cultivate our potential. We are fearfully and wonderfully made (Ps. 139:14), and God has a purpose for us. We should walk in this purpose with joy and contentment, experiencing the peace of God rather than listening to the whispers of past transgressions and mistakes. God said He removed our sins from us as far as the east is from the west (Ps. 103:12). Stop dedicating time in your life to reliving and recalling something you or someone has done that God Almighty Himself forgave and forgot.

Summary

Our nature, upbringing, and the situations we have experienced may have predisposed us to live a sinful life, but the grace of God provided a way for us to be reborn. Take full advantage of that rebirth, leaning on God's Spirit to help you resist temptation, and walk faithfully in His mandates. Growth and maturity in God take time and effort, but the more we yield to God and resist the enemy, the less influence he has on our thoughts and actions. Do not be fearful of making mistakes and sinning. Instead, be conscious of the temptation to sin and the ability to make mistakes and create a lifestyle and mentality that keep our feet from straying. We should not pride ourselves in our sins, allowing them to lead us down paths to destruction. Recognize the immaturity and harm in using God's grace as a license to sin. We must continuously ask God to cleanse and heal us of our messes and mistakes and receive His forgiveness so that condemnation and guilt do not lead us down the long, unpleasant roads to self-loathing. Instead, choose to walk the path of rehabilitation with God. Receive the forgiveness that God freely offers and walk in the grace that He freely gives.

PART 4

Treatment and Prevention

COMMUNICATION

God observes and watches over each of us, and He truly knows what would bring each of us peace, happiness, smoother transitions, and fulfillment of our potential. He desires wholeness for us because He delights in the growth, development, and accomplishments of His children, just like any proud parent. He is a loving parent that encourages and supports us no matter what state we are in or the failures we may have experienced. God has equipped us and wants to teach us how to achieve a good life, one that is not manipulated and darkened by the enemy's influence. After receiving salvation, we become a part of a family. A unit that loves and looks out for our well-being and that we can care for and help in return.

We will discuss nine of the Christian disciplines that develop and guide us into having a healthy relationship with God and those around us. These disciplines are prayer, Bible study, worship, witnessing, fellowship, service, giving, fasting, and mediation. These disciplines equip and enable us to function effectively as the Body of Christ and promote our spiritual growth and maturity as a believer. They are life-altering and part of the transformation and renewal process that conditions our mind and prepares us to walk in the will of God (Rom. 12:1–2).

The Christian disciplines are essential because, when practiced, they bless and minister the collective Body of Christ and us as individuals. The disciplines assist in maintaining a healthy Christian lifestyle. They help us focus on the essentials so that the distractions and struggles of life do not pull us into darkness or bondage.

Communication is key to any relationship, and issues in this area can cause disconnect, misunderstandings, and feelings of neglect. Three of the Christian disciplines are ways of communication between God and humanity: prayer, Bible study, and worship.

Prayer

God wants to be a part of every aspect of our lives, and through prayer, we invite Him into our decision-making, situations, issues, achievements, homes, jobs, and relationships. God knows all and can do all, so why do we need to pray? He can act on our behalf without us talking to Him, but as we spoke about earlier, He wants a relationship. God wants to be a partner with us as we live. He will not usurp the power He gave us: the ability and right to choose. He wants us to accept His will and trust and rely on His love and wisdom, but He will not make us. When we pray, we let God know that we want His help, His will, and His grace. We shouldn't take communicating with God for granted; He wants to hear about our wants, desires, and needs. He wants to walk with us through life. Praying encourages us to partner with God, doing as we have been instructed and equipped to do, while God takes care of the rest.

There is no situation when communication with God is not warranted: "Are any of you suffering hardships? You should pray. Are any of you happy? You should sing praises" (James 5:13). God witnesses every detail of our lives, and we should not restrict what we share with God. He wants to rejoice with us in the right things and helps us deal with and overcome the bad. God is ready to offer His strength, and so we are advised in 1 Chronicles, "Search for the Lord and for his strength; continually seek him" (16:11). He wants to give us the grace to handle every part of our lives, not just the parts we allow others to see. There are other influences at work, and God wants us to be aware of the things that come against the believer. He doesn't want us to be ignorant. Matthew 26:41 warns us, "Keep watch and pray so that you will not give in to temptation. For the spirit is willing, but the body is weak!" Accordingly, God wants us prepared to resist and not surrender to the calls of our flesh. As believers, we continuously have a violent and cunning adversary that seeks our demise. God knows this fact and wants us to let Him shelter us from the attacks of the enemy. He wants to strengthen us in and through our struggles. We have the assurance that God will always be there for us, and we must be patient and prayerful in our hope in God: "Rejoice in our confident hope. Be patient in trouble, and keep on praying" (Rom. 12:12).

We should be faithful in our conversations with God, inviting Him into our every day. A life filled with prayer builds character and relationship. The more we talk with God and listen to Him, the more we think and view situations as He does. God wants an intimate relationship with us, and we develop that by communicating with Him. We should discuss our day and circumstances with Him, listening and seeing what He will impart to us. Scripture tells us that "the Lord is close to all who call on him, yes, to all who call on him in truth" (Ps. 145:18). Prayer strengthens our relationship and our walk for this reason.

Bible Study

Scripture gives us the answers. God's Word directs us on how to be stable and firmly grounded through the highs and lows of life. A believer needs to do more than talk about faith and recite the Word of God; a child of God needs to live their faith and apply His Word. Maintaining a healthy, grounded life is hard with hazy understandings, mottos, and churchy catchphrases. Sitting and being ministered to for thirty to forty-five minutes on Sunday is not enough. We must take the time to know God for ourselves so that our relationship can have depth and meaning. God knows our every thought, even the number of hair on our heads. How much do we know about Him beyond His love that saves and blesses us? Do we know His likes and dislikes, His nature and desires? Do we know about His character? God wants more than for us to ask for things without inquiring how He feels on a subject or what He thinks about a situation. A good relationship is about taking responsibility and doing your part, and our role in our relationship with God is laid out in His Word. If we do not study it, how will we ever know what our part is and how to do it?

Crying Out but Not Listening and Doing

"So why do you keep calling me 'Lord, Lord!' when you don't do what I say? I will show you what it's like when someone comes to me, listens to my teaching, and then follows it. It is like a person building a house who digs deep and lays the foundation on solid rock. When the floodwaters rise and break against that house, it stands firm because it is well built" (Luke 6:46–48).

Jesus called out those who followed Him around, asking for instruction and wisdom and not applying it to their lives. They would call on Him but would not listen or implement any of the principles that He taught. Jesus wanted the cycle to stop and for His followers to realize their responsibility in the Messiah-believer relationship. He instructed them on how to deal with their situations and how to have a full life, but they would never understand and apply the words to their lives. Studying the Word helps us ingrain God's principles and teachings in our hearts so that we will not be ignorant and disobedient in this way (Ps. 119:11). We, as believers, should have a love for God that prompts us to please Him. God takes pleasure when we truly understand His Word and can adequately explain His truths (2 Tim. 2:15).

God does not want us confused and anxious. He lets us know who He is in His Word: "Do not stifle the Holy Spirit.

Do not scoff at prophecies, but test everything that is said. Hold on to what is good. Stay away from every kind of evil" (1 Thess. 5:19–22). God wants us to have confidence in His Spirit so that we won't hinder God's effort in our lives and the lives of others. We gain this confidence through knowing His Word. When we know what is righteous, we can compare what we are uncertain about with God's Word. When things do not align with the Word of God, we can confidently reject them. When we can confirm something through the Word of God, we can confidently apply it and walk in it (Acts 17:11). Listen to what people and preachers say, then study it for yourself to make sure it aligns with the Word of God. We are not to blindly follow leadership but to equip ourselves to sincerely and loyally follow God. We should honor those in leadership, but we should not follow them on paths that run contrary to the will of God.

Studying the Word of God requires some technique so that a believer doesn't become overwhelmed or confused. Much of the Word of God is straightforward, but we can sometimes struggle to translate what we read into applicable knowledge. There are no rules that we must follow to study the Word of God, but we should always look for context. It is a good practice to read a little before and a little after the verse or verses of Scripture that one is studying to draw the proper understanding and conclusions. Some parts of the Bible may seem daunting, but with the aid of the Holy Spirit and credible commentaries, we can gain knowledge and understanding in our private Bible study. Apply yourself so that the time invested, large or small, produces enrichment and learning.

Worship

Worship shows God that you honor and acknowledge that no one greater exists in all the universe. Worship requires more than words. Honoring God translates into a lifestyle. God orchestrates and controls all things, and the believer should be happy and empowered by the knowledge. Truly knowing God should instill a reverence for God in our thoughts, activities, and plans. When we genuinely believe that God is the most excellent and powerful being, we view life and respond to its situations differently. We tell of God's goodness so that others will recognize His greatness and honor and fear Him (1 Chron. 16:28–31). We speak about the works of His hands so that others will see who He is and worship Him too. But most of all, we worship Him because He is God. We honor Him and are thankful for who He is and the great things He has done and will do.

Worship is reserved only for God. He is the only one worthy of worship (Exod. 20:2–5a). He not only created us but also loves us and involves himself in our lives despite our depravity. He loved us in our bondage and delivered us from slavery to sin. He rescued us from an unprofitable life that would only bring death, and He gave us an eternity that holds promise and joy everlasting. For humanity, and especially the believer, to elevate something or someone above God, whether it is in their priority, fear, reverence, or praise, is to anger God. He created and provided it all: our worship of Him is only the proper response. He has rescued us from enemies, healed us, gave opportunities, brought about deliverance and peace. Who wouldn't want to worship a God like Him except the ungrateful? Even in bad times, God remains omnipotent and merciful. He is always worthy of praise, and we should worship Him.

Moreover, we should worship God for who He is, not only for what He does. In the book of Daniel, Shadrach, Meshach, and Abednego recognized that God could save them, and they resolved to worship only God even if He chose not to deliver them (3:16–18). True worshippers don't only praise God when things go well. They decided to honor and worship Him during the mediocre, hard, and difficult times in their lives. The Hebrew boys in the book of Daniel knew who their God was. They did not hesitate to worship Him and deny all others in the face of death. They understood that even martyrdom did not lessen God's greatness. The Hebrew boys refused to worship any other God; they knew their God, and their circumstances did not change their faith in Him. Believers today should take that attitude about worship. We should know that no experience can diminish God's power or His love for us. A painful event or challenging situation does not make God unworthy of honor and praise; it is just an opportunity to look beyond the circumstance to see an awesome God who cares and wants to provide healing and deliverance.

Once we can look beyond the obstacles to see an awesome God, we can worship Him by accepting the truth and living an honorable life. During Jesus's encounter with the Samaritan woman at the well, she wanted to discuss the proper place of worship. Once she realized Jesus had a relationship with God, she listened, and Jesus took the time to educate her on what was important when it comes to worship. He shared with her, "The time is coming—indeed it's here now—when true worshipers will worship the Father in spirit and in truth. The Father is looking for those who will worship him that way. For God is Spirit, so those who worship him must worship in spirit and in truth" (John 4:23–24). God does not put any physical stipulation on acceptable worship. However, we are to worship Him from our spirit, not a place of mental obligation, but a place where we connect with Him in reverence and honor. We praise Him, grateful for who He is and the great things He has done. We do not have to fabricate and dream up reasons to worship Him. We worship Him by accepting the truth and living a life that honors Him.

The best way to worship God in our daily lives is to give ourselves to Him (Rom. 12:1–2). We honor Him in our lifestyle by yielding ourselves to be transformed. We transform from a person who allows the standards of this fallen world to determine and influence our life to one who surrenders those mentalities for the mind of Christ. When we learn the will of God and perform it, we worship through obedience. God adopted us and became our Father, but we get lazy in that blessed position, and we can lose our reverence and fear of who God is. Hebrews 12:28–29 says, "Since we are receiving a Kingdom that is unshakable, let us be thankful and please God by worshiping him with holy fear and awe. For our God is a devouring fire." Let us not get so accustomed to God's love, provision, and grace that we are no longer grateful for them. We should not allow the trials of this world to persuade us in discounting and devaluing the tremendous blessings God gives us.

Summary

The Christian disciplines of communication are significant in the lives of the believer. Once we have confidence in our relationship with God, our relationship with the rest of the Body of Christ and the world becomes more manageable. God gave us prayer, study, and worship to connect with Him. When we invite God into our lives and decision-making, we develop an intimate relationship with Him. God tells us that as we draw near to Him, He comes nearer to us. This nearness allows us to receive, understand, and do God's will through His grace. We are not only to communicate with Him but also interact with those around us. It is His will for the Body of Christ to have an intimate relationship with one another through community.

COMMUNITY

A believer not only has a relationship with God but also fosters relationships with the community of believers and prospective believers. The Body of Christ is here to nurture, teach, support, minister, and encourage one another. He has equipped each believer with gifts, ministries, and skills for the Body, and by practicing the four Christian disciplines of community, you strengthen yourself along with those around you. It can be hard to see the beauty of community when our society emphasizes individuality so much. God made us all unique, but He did so to show the beauty of all those differences when they work together in harmony, like a rainbow. It was not for separation, isolation, or idolization of one group over another. The enemy would have people focus on differences to create discord rather than acknowledging the strength and blessing of diversity—differences avail opportunities to make resounding improvements and positive impact on people's lives. The enemy would like us to view them as reasons for entitlement or cause for isolation and separation, which benefits his plans of attack.

God's Word speaks of community frequently because it is vital to the Christian walk. The Body of Christ must work together, strengthening, supporting, encouraging, nurturing, defending, and teaching one another. The greatest among the kingdoms of God are servers (Matt. 23:11), which we should all be. Those who consider and think of others' needs while trusting God to meet theirs are those who are truly fulfilled and truly fulfill their purpose. Jesus's life on this earth depicted the actions and mentality of a server. As the Messiah, he did not cater to the needs of people because they deserved it but purely because they needed it and He could provide it. When handing out blessings and deliverance, He only withheld from those who wouldn't receive. Jesus did what others could not do for themselves, but He never handicapped them by doing what they could do. Jesus did not use His deity as a way to avoid serving. Instead, He used His position as a means of helping others and using every opportunity to make a difference and show humanity a better way.

Witnessing

Witnessing becomes a part of the believer's life when they become a Christian. Their lives are on display, and people begin to attribute their actions, attitudes, and conversations to Christianity, whether rightly so or not. The believer represents the Body of Christ and the invisible kingdom of God. As representatives, we must be mindful of what we are portraying to the world. Paul tells us that we are letters for the world to read. He writes, "Clearly, you are a letter from Christ showing the result of our ministry among you. This 'letter' is written not with pen and ink but with the Spirit of the living God. It is carved not on tablets of stone, but on human hearts" (2 Cor. 3:3). God has a lot of things that He wants to share with the world. We, as letters from God to the world, depict and share God's love, grace, and deliverance to the world through our lives. The believer does not need to become anxious or wary about this new position but should rest in the confidence of Christ. By honoring Christ in our lives, we invite others to want to know about our relationship with Him and our salvation.

For this reason, Paul advises, "You must worship Christ as Lord of your life. And if someone asks about your hope as a believer, always be ready to explain it" (1 Pet. 3:15). We, as believers, must prepare ourselves to answer these questions and explain the love and sacrifice of Christ. After we receive the good news of our salvation through Christ's death and resurrection, we are to share the sweet perfume of God's Word to others. And because we know God's Word, we understand that some may not rejoice about the good news. The gospel's message is a sweet fragrance to those who are ready to receive the works of Christ on the cross but a death sentence to those who do not (2 Cor. 2:14–27). Those who are not open to salvation will turn up their noses to it because the Word of God only proclaims their upcoming judgment and damnation. However, for those whose hearts have been prepared to receive the good news, the Word is a sweet fragrance that speaks life to their souls. Paul tells us in Romans, "For I am not ashamed of this Good News about Christ. It is the power of God at work, saving everyone who believes—the Jew first and also the Gentile" (Rom. 1:16). Like Paul, we should not be ashamed that we believe in the good news because sharing it is the only way to make a real, everlasting difference in the lives of those around us. Once we share the good news and lift Christ in our lives for others to see, we do not have to worry about how, when, or if they will receive our witness. The rest is up to God. God draws others to us to change their heart. Our responsibility is to present a good witness, an excellent testament, and then allow others to read and hear the letter that God composed with our lives. Paul tells us that one will do the sowing and another may do the watering, but God gives the increases (1 Cor. 3:6–7). We, as believers, are commanded to do our part and witness. God will take care of the rest, utilizing His Spirit to bring forth any fruit or change in an individual's life.

As witnesses and representatives, we must be aware of ourselves and ensure we put forth our best, honest effort. God does not require perfection to be a witness, but He does want the believer to have a moral standard for how they live their lives. He wants the believer to walk in love so that others can truly see and understand the kingdom of God. The believer should not get caught up in bickering and distasteful behavior when others do not graciously accept their witness. For example, 2 Timothy remarks, "A servant of the Lord must not quarrel but must be kind to everyone, be able to teach, and be patient with difficult people" (2:24). We witness to a dying world so that others come to understand and receive the truth of salvation. We do it not for publicity, accomplishment, or monetary aspirations; "we are not like the many hucksters who preach for personal profit. We preach the Word of God with sincerity and with Christ's authority, knowing that God is watching us" (2 Cor. 2:17). Let us, as believers, be earnest witnesses to the world so that we work to strengthen the community of believers instead of casting a dark shadow on it or scaring people away.

Fellowship

Fellowship in the Body of Christ refers to supporting and encouraging fellow believers. Some think of fellowship as an activity that should take minimal effort. We say "Hi" and casually ask about one another but do not invest too much time or brain space to another person's affairs. However, Paul tells us to "love each other with genuine affection, and take delight in honoring each other" (Rom. 12:10). When we fellowship with another believer, we should genuinely take an interest in their well-being and support them in any way that God deems necessary. We are the Body of Christ, God's hands and feet, and we must look past what we ask from God and see how we can answer someone else's prayer (Heb 10:24–25).

We must look after and support our fellow believers. If we turn a blind eye to one another's struggles, we are guilty of dereliction of duty. We willfully let our fellow believers flounder in their struggles when we could have shown support. Support doesn't mean you know the solutions to their problems or that you are the solution to their problems. Support means you allow someone to lean on you in times of struggle and weakness. Support is encouraging and being helpful when possible. Take the time to pray with others for solutions, blessings, guidance, deliverance, and healing as they go through difficult times. We don't stop praying until they receive their answer. We pray without ceasing for their provision, wisdom, and protection as they flourish in the good times. Fellowship also requires the believer to share faith, along with greetings and struggles. By sharing God's Word and our victories with one another, we help encourage and support one another:

> Is there any encouragement from belonging to Christ? Any comfort from his love? Any fellowship together in the Spirit? Are your hearts tender and compassionate? Then make me truly happy by agreeing wholeheartedly with each other, loving one another, and working together with one mind and purpose. (Phil. 2:1–2)

As Paul implies above, God wants the Body of Christ unified, but it is impossible to sync up with others if we do not communicate. In fellowship, we learn to work together. We get over differences and agree on common goals and purposes. When we come together, we can have an everlasting impact on our communities, establishing programs and outreaches that enlighten people about Christ and meet another's needs. Jesus speaks about the power of unity and how it can open the eyes of those who have yet to realize and acknowledge God's love: "I am in them, and you are in me. May they experience such perfect unity that the world will know that you sent me and that you love them as much as you love me" (John 17:23). Some introverts may see fellowship as daunting and overwhelming. However, we must realize that God did not ask us to do anything that isn't beneficial to us. God already established a common thread through the believers who are parts of the Body of Christ. This common thread is the basis of our fellowship with God and one another (1 John 1:7). God's Spirit guides us in this fellowship with one another, leading us to avoid discord and sin while establishing a common ground with acts of love.

Service

The Word of God shows us repeatedly how much God values the heart of service. Jesus gives us numerous examples of how to meet the needs of others and how service is an honorable undertaking. He asks, "Who is more important, the one who sits at the table or the one who serves? The one who sits at the table, of course. But not here! For I am among you as one who serves" (Luke 22:27). Jesus talks to the disciples and tells them that the world's perspective is not God's perspective. Jesus not only says that serving is important but also shows it by coming to this earth to serve. It is through service that we cater to the needs of the world and make a lasting change. He wants His body to follow His example and embrace the mentality of a servant seeking the betterment of others, of service. Jesus lets us know that a servant is the highest position anyone can hold in the kingdom of God (Matt. 23:11). While I was growing up, service to others became second nature because my mother always volunteered and took us along to help with something. I did not think much of it; it was just something I was supposed to do, so I did it. Not until I was older did I begin to recognize that people had different opinions about service. Some people praised and encouraged my sisters and me for our acts of service, while others would offer judgment. Some would go as far as to take advantage of our volunteering and make us personal servants or errand runners. However, I already established a mind for serving, and the opposing mentalities of others never swayed it.

God allowed me to recognize that those who were unpleasant or who took advantage of my willingness to serve had the issue, not me. He also showed me that I did not have to make other people's issues mine. Their negativity or their desire to exploit others should not discourage me from what we are created to do as the Body of Christ serves others. Nothing is wrong with helping others, and those who have skewed opinions on it need prayer, not judgment. To this day, I am grateful that my mother instilled a servant's heart into her children.

Meeting the needs of others shines light in their darkness. We are told in Isaiah, "Feed the hungry, and help those in trouble. Then your light will shine out from the darkness, and the darkness around you will be as bright as noon" (Isa. 58:10). We can become the light that the person needs and reveal to them God, who moves through us on their behalf. When we serve others, we serve God. God sees the need of the poor and oppressed. He hears the cries for help, and when we answer those cries and bless others, we honor God's promise to provide for His people and "rain on the just as well as the unjust."

Matthew 25:35–36, 40 shows us how God feels about our acts of service; it touches Him personally:

> For I was hungry, and you fed me. I was thirsty, and you gave me a drink. I was a stranger, and you invited me into your home. I was naked, and you gave me clothing. I was sick, and you cared for me. I was in prison, and you visited me. And the King will say, "I tell you the truth when you did it to one of the least of these my brothers and sisters, you were doing it to me!"

God has called us to have a servant's heart and make a difference in the lives of others through acts of kindness. The parable of the Good Samaritan shows what a difference someone can make when they go out of their way to care. We do not have to know the people we are helping or benefit from helping them. We are to honor God by opening ourselves to meet the need that we see. Paul writes in 2 Corinthians, "Two good things will result from this ministry of giving—the needs of the believers in Jerusalem will be met, and they will joyfully express their thanks to God. As a result of your ministry, they will give glory to God. For your generosity to them and all believers will prove that you are obedient to the Good News of Christ" (9:12–13). Through meeting the needs of people, we bring God glory. We honor Him and His call to love. Through these acts of kindness and compassion, others can see what it indeed looks like to live for God and embrace the good news. It is life-changing not only to those who readily receive it but also to those who encounter those giving believers.

Moreover, good deeds breathe life into your faith. It makes the things you believe manifest into action—something tangible that others can experience. James let us know in chapter 2, verse 26 that our faith is like a lifeless body without good works. Just as a body without breath has no potential for life and purpose, faith without good works is useless. It is there but brings no benefit to the person the has it or the situation they are in.

Our actions show us where we stand in our faith. If we do that which we believe, it reveals that our relationship with God is more than words but commitment. We can tell people how great God is and how life-changing it is to receive salvation, but if we do not use any of the gifts and talents that God gives us to better the lives of others, how will they ever experience it and desire to know God for themselves? Our platitudes and reassurances to others are lifeless, useless; our words are followed by action. When we read and speak and do not act, it tells the world that the Word of God is okay to discuss but it is not to be embraced or applied. God's Word in the eyes of the world becomes cliché with no power or purpose. Faith in God is more than receiving from him; it is about using what we have to help others so that they may also experience Him through us. Scripture says, "Now someone may argue, 'Some people have faith; others have good deeds.' But I say, 'How can you show me your faith if you don't have good deeds? I will show you my faith by my good deeds'" (James 2:18). In other words,

God wants us to be more than mouthpieces; He wants us to be examples, light, and salt to those around us. We cannot do that with words alone. Jesus did more than just share His words to set people free; he put those words into action by ministering to others and walking in the love and will of God.

We should also know that this service to God and His Kingdom is remembered and rewarded.

> For God is not unjust. He will not forget how hard you have worked for him and how you have shown your love to him by caring for other believers, as you still do. Our great desire is that you will keep on loving others as long as life lasts, in order to make certain that what you hope for will come true. Then you will not become spiritually dull and indifferent. Instead, you will follow the example of those who are going to inherit God's promises because of their faith and endurance. (Heb. 6:10–12)

God sees the believers' work, and He sees the time, the effort, and the resources they use to help others. God values the believer's acts of service, which nurture hope in those who look to God for provision. They ward off indifference by caring for others. When we put ourselves in a position to serve others, we, as believers, need to tap into the fruit and power of the Holy Spirit. So long as we make a habit of drawing on Him to help us, we do not allow ourselves to lay stagnant, but we stir up that which is within us. Let us not just talk of faith and endurance but also be examples of it for others.

Even in service, we must use wisdom to understand boundaries and limitations. We are to give of ourselves in a manner that allows us to maintain a healthy emotional, mental, physical, and spiritual life. We are not to push ourselves beyond that which we have prepared or ordained to handle. If our physical, emotional, mental, and spiritual life become imbalanced or depleted, we need to rest, re-evaluate, and seek wisdom on how to establish or re-establish a healthy way of serving others. We, as a part of the Body of Christ, should positively influence our community, but service does not call for us to suffer in the other areas of our life. When you find that something does not work or no longer works, then you should address it. Jesus took breaks and escaped from the crowd so that He did not suffer unduly. Service is admirable, and we are all called to it, but zeal without wisdom is harmful even with this Christian discipline. Let us be faithful in asking God for direction, understanding, and strength and taking the time to receive it while showing others the love of Christ through service.

Giving

As believers, we must give because we are God's hands and feet. We are there to meet the needs of God's people. The actions of a giver bless both the receiver and the giver. Proverbs gives us a lot of wisdom on how giving works and the benefits of giving. The proper heart of a giver should not be proud or willing to condescend to the less fortunate, which is unacceptable to God (Prov. 14:21). The giver should be generous without holding back what could help or benefit another (Prov. 11:25, 3:27). We should not allow greed to taint our hearts for giving (Prov. 21:26). The believer is to be a champion and a voice that speaks up for the justice of the poor and helpless (Prov. 31:9). God wants us to honor Him with not only the things that have become useless to us but also the best that we have (Prov. 3:9). We are to "give freely and become more wealthy; be stingy and lose everything" (Prov. 11:24). Giving opens up doors to the giver and blesses them to be in a position where influential people will work on their behalf (Prov. 18:16).

Giving does not come easily to some, but that doesn't mean one cannot learn to love giving. If we do not have the ministry of giving, that does not exempt us from the practice of giving. We can pray that God gives us the grace to give. By giving, we avail ourselves to not only be a blessing but to also be blessed. We are advised, "Give, and you will receive. Your gift will return to you in full—pressed down, shaken together to make room for more, running over, and poured into your lap. The amount you give will determine the amount you get back" (Luke 6:38). When we do not practice giving, we not only keep others from a blessing but also hold back seeds for future benefits. Giving follows the principles of sowing and reaping.

When a person isn't a giver, it doesn't disqualify them from being blessed, but it does influence their potential to reap. God doesn't want the believer giving from a place of pressure, resentment, or anger, but He does call the believer to provide.

We must bring our giving practices to God in prayer so that we can offer from a grateful heart: "You must each decide in your heart how much to give. And don't give reluctantly or in response to pressure. 'For God loves a person who gives cheerfully'" (2 Cor. 9:7). God has a tender spot for those who share in His joy of giving. God gives not to receive something back but to influence our lives positively. We should be happy that we have the opportunity to meet a need and bring about a positive change.

The structure and order of services of a church may vary, but the mission and purpose of the church have not changed. The church is an organization of believers who unite to honor God and spread the good news. They come together to encourage the body and to bring healing to a dying world. Some like to believe that it should be a free enterprise; however, the church cannot give what it does not have, and the church only has what the members of the body provide. We should not devalue the ministries and workers of God by thinking that they do not deserve a wage for their dedicated time and service to the body. If we do not support the needs of the church, it can't function adequately or accomplish the missions of God. God blesses us so that we can bless others and meet their needs. God has no issue with blessing the believer, and He has put in place the principle of sowing and reaping so that the believer does not become selfish but sees the beauty and power of giving. The book of Matthew says, "Do to others whatever you would like them to do to you. This is the essence of all that is taught in the law and the prophets" (7:12). Likewise, we cannot let the vice of greed hinder our growth and purpose. We can combat it with the love and grace of God to show the enemy just how much earthly goods and wealth of this world compares to the glorious wealth of walking in God's Spirit. Instead of storing up worldly wealth, we should listen to Matthew 6:20–21, which says, "Store your treasures in heaven, where moths and rust cannot destroy, and thieves do not break in and steal. Wherever your treasure is, there the desires of your heart will also be." When we do give, we should give in secret, without seeking another's praise. If we work for recognition, then we have received our reward and should not look to God for another (Matt. 6:1). The believer should give solely to meet a need and honor God. As a part of the Body of Christ, we are here to build up, strengthen, and take care of one another. Family members do not help one another for praise; we give hoping that we can make the lives of a loved one better.

Summary

Community is how the Body of Christ supports and encourages one another. Fellowship, service, and giving are Christian disciplines we all need to implement in our lives. We should pray for the grace to walk in them with love and humility. Community is a powerful construct that can unite the body and keep the enemy at bay. We function as the hands and feet of Christ by meeting the needs of those around us through our support, time, encouragement, and resources. When we serve in this way, we help heal, grow, enlighten, and strengthen others. If the Body of Christ does not provide this type of support and aid its members and the world, they will find a tainted version of it that will lead them away into darkness. Everyone needs help and support at different times in their lives, and the Body of Christ should be ready as a community to minister to those in need as God has ordained.

DEDICATION

Dedication requires self-control, and self-control allows the believer to move freely without the influence of vices, emotions, or circumstances. Self-control empowers us to remove the weight of uncertainty when we act or react, and it grounds us in character and promises of God. Events will still disrupt our journey, but the focus that comes with self-control allows us to see beyond the problems to solutions. The last two disciplines we will discuss require us to devote ourselves to a goal and to utilize restraint. These disciplines are fasting and meditation, disciplines that develop our spiritual strength and understanding. Fasting and meditation require us to look beyond our initial wants, desires, and reactions and to seek God for guidance. They focus on what we need to do while submitting everything else to God. Fasting and meditation bring clarity of vision by focusing on God, the Source of it all. These disciplines help look beyond our limited scope to God, who can open our spiritual understanding. Fasting and meditation help us grasp what our physical eyes cannot comprehend.

Fasting

Fasting can be a daunting discipline for some. We sometimes respond to it like a spoiled child who throws a fit when told that they cannot have what they want. Fasting is uncomfortable, and surrendering to the cries of the flesh are tempting to quiet it. Fasting can be a hard discipline to establish, but God does not call the believer to do something that He will not support and empower them to do. Fasting helps the believer re-establish control, that they may have lost to habit and indulgence. God calls us to fast, and He places stipulations on it so that we know when it is being misused or perverted. He calls us to fast with hearts that are committed to honoring and glorifying Him. In Isaiah, God reprimands the children of Israel because their performance of religious acts such as fasting was for show and did not mean enough to them to take it to heart. They wanted God to move on their behalf because they adhered to God's mandates. Instead, He called them out for their unfaithful hearts. Their unmovable hearts and ungodly ways revealed that their type of fasting did not bring any benefit to their spiritual growth or their relationship with God. They did not honor Him, and He was not pleased with their mentality toward what was supposed to be dedicated time to Him.

> Yet they act so pious! They come to the Temple every day and seem delighted to learn all about me. They act like a righteous nation that would never abandon the laws of its God. They ask me to take action on

their behalf, pretending they want to be near me. 'We have fasted before you!' they say. 'Why aren't you impressed? We have been very hard on ourselves, and you don't even notice it!' "I will tell you why!" I respond. "It's because you are fasting to please yourselves. Even while you fast, you keep oppressing your workers." (Isa. 58: 2–3)

When we fast, we should not do so in pride or for recognition, as do the children of Israel in this passage. We should fast humbly and earnestly, seeking God to intercede on our behalf and the behalf of others. In seeking God, we should lay aside sinful, displeasing ways because fasting is not about depriving the physical body of food and pleasure. It is also about controlling the flesh and our sinful nature. We cannot fast and knowingly sin.

We fast so that we can focus on the voice of God with a more receptive and undistracted mind. In our lives, and especially during fasting, we should not allow our flesh to control our thoughts, feelings, or actions. It can be hard to do at times because just as the physical body calls out for food or pleasure, our sinful nature cries out and throws tantrums without being fed. When we do not feed our physical bodies, they weaken, and it is the same with the voice of sin. The screamed demands of the flesh begin to quiet when it is not fed, and the believer can hear God more clearly. In Isaiah 58, God not only tells them what they did wrong but also shares what fasting truly is about:

No, this is the kind of fasting I want: Free those who are wrongly imprisoned; lighten the burden of those who work for you. Let the oppressed go free and remove the chains that bind people. Share your food with the hungry, and give shelter to the homeless. Give clothes to those who need them, and do not hide from relatives who need your help.

Remove the heavy yoke of oppression. Stop pointing your finger and spreading vicious rumors! Feed the hungry and help those in trouble. (Isaiah 58:6–7, 9b–10a)

Fasting is not about being seen or heard by God but honoring God and making a righteous difference in the world around you. It is not a stagnant practice of deprivation but an active, moving practice of building, delivering, providing, and setting free. Fasting is a commitment to make a positive change in us and around us. It is about yielding ourselves to God for ministration and availing ourselves to minister to others. God wants us to walk humbly in His spirit of love and to follow his guidance rather than our instinct. Many times, He leads us to help someone else

When my son was three years old, he asked me, "When is God going to come down? When are we going to see Him?" At first, I could not come up with a sufficient-enough answer, so I told him God is everywhere. We just can't see Him, but He is there and can see us. My son asked the question again a couple of weeks later, and I thought about it and gave him this answer:

"God sees you and is everywhere, and He loves you so much. He gave you a daddy and mommy to take care of you and love you. He also gave you teachers to teach you all the things He wants you to know. God is not going to come down here and physically let you see Him, but He is watching you and knows about everything you need, so He sends people and angels to take care of you because He loves you. We can't see the angels, but they keep you safe and do what God tells them to do for you." I shared that to say you, the believer, are the answers to other people's prayers. We honor God by fasting from what we want and taking the time to make a positive difference in someone else's life on God's behalf.

When we fast, we lay aside our worries and give all our cares, grievances, and requests to God. We learn more about Him and His plans. We stop thinking about ourselves and let God gather the angels and people we need to act on our behalf. We are God's hands and feet, and through fasting we prepare ourselves to be a blessing to others and receive from God. God goes on to tell us in Isaiah 58 what He will do for the people who fast, how He has called them to fast:

> Then your salvation will come like the dawn, and your wounds will quickly heal. Your godliness will lead you forward, and the glory of the Lord will protect you from behind. Then when you call, the Lord will answer. "Yes, I am here," he will quickly reply...
> Then your light will shine out from the darkness, and the darkness around you will be as bright as noon.

The Lord will guide you continually, giving you water when you are dry and restoring your strength. You will be like a well-watered garden, like an ever-flowing spring. Some of you will rebuild the deserted ruins of your cities. Then you will be known as a rebuilder of walls and a restorer of homes. (Isaiah 58:8–9a,10b–12)

As this passage attests, fasting can heal our wounds and allows the Spirit of God to lead us forward in our walk with Christ and the presence of God. Because we placed ourselves in God's hand and His will, when we call on Him, we can trust He will answer. Fasting allows the light of God to shine through us brightly, bringing clarity and understanding to our situations. We place ourselves in a position to be restored and strengthened with fasting. God wants us to be like the tree planted beside still waters, getting everything we need from Him. When we root ourselves near the flow of His Spirit, we will be renewed and will receive power to restore things in our lives and the lives of others.

How does fasting differ from the everyday Christian lifestyle of loving God and your fellow believer? Isaiah 58:1 instructs us on how dedication looks to God: "Keep the Sabbath day holy. Don't pursue your own interests on that day but enjoy the Sabbath and speak of it with delight as the Lord's holy day. Honor the Sabbath in everything you do on that day, and don't follow your own desires or talk idly." Fasting is a consecrated time. As the Sabbath day is a time designated for rest in God, fasting is a time to change our focus from dealing with the day-to-day to experiencing the day with God. During fasting, the emphasis of our day changes from getting through the week in a way that honors God to actively avoiding distractions so that we can dedicate time to talking, listening, and thinking about Him and His will. When fasting, we put forth a concentrated effort to keep ourselves in line. We do this by praying, worshipping, and reading the Bible more often. We intentionally spend time with God during our day and stay away from things that lead us into selfish or idle behavior. We avoid actions, places, and situations that would please us rather than please God. We stay away from distracting behaviors that hinder our time with God. God doesn't mind us finding pleasure in life, yet fasting is a time of dedication, a time that we set aside to please Him. Fasting doesn't always mean that we have to separate from the world around us. Sometimes, fasting calls for us to immerse ourselves in godly works while God deals with our hearts and situation; both ways honor God. In times of fasting, adding or subtracting things from our lives can profit us, our relationship with God, and the Body of Christ. When we fast, we should look for God's guidance in how we should go about it so that we do not waste our time but instead bring honor to God and benefit to us.

Meditation (Solitude)

Meditation is something we all do naturally; we think and ponder about people and situations and even make up things to consider and worry about throughout the day. Meditating as a Christian discipline is beneficial because we actively create a positive and productive narrative on which to think. We are to hand our worries to God and rest in His peace (Isa. 26:3). Meditating requires the believer to put aside other concerns and consciously ponder on the things of God instead. We set aside time to focus and ground ourselves in God's Word and His presence. We allow ourselves to bathe our minds with His truths, His promises, and His purpose. Ultimately, meditation brings about resolution, peace, deliverance, growth, and success, which is why the book of Joshua advises, "Study this Book of Instruction continually. Meditate on it day and night so you will be sure to obey everything written in it. Only then will you prosper and succeed in all you do" (1:8). We succeed by learning and following the instruction of God. These principles are gained not only by reading them but also by thinking on them regularly, meditating on them until they become our way of thinking. It's like a player learning the playbook and practicing it so that they know what they can do to stop their opponent and score after the game starts. We cannot expect ourselves to obey everything in the Word of God or pull off the plays if we do not know the content or have it memorized.

Meditating on God's Word is like building muscle memory. We read and think about His Word so much that the proper response automatically presents itself when a situation arises, and then we are left to choose to do it or the opposite. In some cases, we must reinforce muscle memory with intentional thoughts and actions. Meditation on God's Word makes our normal reaction more prone to be a righteous one. Meditating on God's Word reinforces our resolve to do what is right. It is a way to tap into the life-giving source inside so that it can flow through us, refreshing, empowering, maturing, and directing us to do what is right.

When we set aside time to spend with God, God rewards us for it. We are told this fact in Matthew 6:6, which says, "When you pray, go away by yourself, shut the door behind you, and pray to your Father in private. Then your Father, who sees everything, will reward you." While we spend time with God, we can see His will clearly and receive what He has for us with an understanding heart and open arms. Moreover, we can reinforce our resolve to honor Him and follow Christ when we meditate and concentrate on God's presence and Word. This time of meditation strengthens and heals us. Proverbs tells us, "My child, pay attention to what I say. Listen carefully to my words. Don't lose sight of them. Let them penetrate deep into your heart, for they bring life to those who find them, and healing to their whole body" (4:20–22). God's Word holds power, life-giving power. We are revived and made whole by meditating and heeding His Word. We should think about all the good that is around us because we can find God in not only His Word but also every aspect of our lives. We, as believers, need to realize that God has not forsaken us to this wicked world. We need to take time to find the beauty He has left in it for us to enjoy. He still shows His love and grace and beauty through people, places, things, and situations. The enemy would like us to get bogged down in the bad so that we forget to see the good. But the good is out there. God is moving not just through the Word but in and around the lives of His creation.

Summary

Participating in the disciplines of fasting and meditation takes dedication and self-control. These practices ground us so that we can knowledgeably and effectively function in the will of God. These disciplines call us to set aside self and look to God and His word. Fasting and meditation are to be devoted to intentional time with God. This time is for us to not only honor God but also align ourselves with God so that we may receive from Him. Through fasting and meditation, we show God and ourselves that we prioritize staying connected and aligned with Him. We reject the desires and reasoning of this world and resist the pull of the flesh. We put forth a conscious effort to focus on God and the things of God. Practicing fasting and meditation demonstrates that our connection with God is more than what we can receive from Him. It is also in how we are willing to honor Him through relationship. When we put forth a dedicated effort to learn and walk in the ways of God, we will see God's hand in our lives. We fast and meditate knowing that only what God thinks and speaks holds in every situation. We cherish the Word of God because we know they hold love, power, deliverance, opportunity, and purpose.

CONCLUSION

God created us for a relationship with Him, and we, as the Body of Christ, are a testament to His infinite love and wisdom. God values relationships with His creations so much that He gave His Son, Jesus, so that He could re-establish an intimate relationship with humanity. The purpose, provision, and instruction that God gave Adam and Eve in the garden attested that God's motives for humanity have always been to bless, protect, and commune with them. However, God gave us free will so that we can decide what kind of relationship we want with Him and what kind of life we want to lead. The fall of humanity changed the state into which we are born, but it did not change God's love or His purpose for us.

After receiving God's gracious gift of salvation, God seals and marks the believer as His with the Holy Spirit so that He can secure them as a part of the kingdom of God and the Body of Christ. Once we are members, we enter into God's refining process that brings growth and healing through transformation. This transformation occurs through the Word of God we learn, the deliverances from bondages and strongholds we gain, the healing of hurts and failures we receive, the cleansing of sin and ungodly mentalities we allow, and the commitment to the will of God that we make. God matures the believer through His Spirit, Word, and circumstances, transforming us into the image of His Son. The process can vary in degrees of comfort, depending on how much we yield ourselves to the guidance and molding of God's hands. Our cooperation and willingness to learn from God determine how much transforming takes place and the amount of abundant life we experience. Laying down the mentality and lust of the world can be hard, but when replaced with the character and will of God, there will be no regrets.

These words are to encourage us to embrace the healing and health that Christ has died to give us, accepting the abundance that comes from the Spirit of God within us. The Spirit of God helps us maintain a healthy, holistic lifestyle that is God-conscious. We are to put on the mind of Christ, allowing God's character and principles to dictate how we handle ourselves. We do this because we want a full, open, and prosperous relationship with God and with others. At the end of our journey on this earth, we desire to hear, "Well done, my good and faithful servant" (Matt. 25:23). And we will hear these words not only because we were victorious in every big and little battle but because we sought Him to make a difference in us as we glorified Him by making a positive difference in the lives of those around us. God equipped us with the power and tools to heal the Body of Christ, and we can choose whether we will be a part of the problem or a part of the solution. We decide each day through our thoughts, words, and deeds if we will contribute to the disease of our body or if we will be agents of healing and growth. We should lay aside our old nature and way of doing things. We should wholeheartedly embrace all the teachings, promises, and gifts of God and walk in the abundant life that we have through Christ.

AFTERWORD

I pray *Healing the Body of Christ* encouraged you to be mindful of your responsibility as a member of the Body of Christ. I hope you become diligent in nurturing your emotional, spiritual, and mental health and realize the importance of utilizing the Word of God and His Spirit to maintain that health. We are children of God and encouraged to work with the Spirit of God to generate healing and growth in our lives and the lives of others. I pray this body of work has presented you with a clear understanding of the principles and tools that God gives us to bring changes that will foster a productive and triumphant Christian lifestyle. I hope this book has stirred you to go a little deeper, grow a little stronger, and grasp a new level of God's provision for healing and victory in your life.

REFERENCES

All Scripture is *New Living Translation,* unless otherwise noted.

Holy Bible, New Living Translation, copyright 1996, 2004, 2015 by Tyndale House Foundation.

Holy Bible, New International Version, NIV, copyright 1973, 1978, 1984, 2011 by Biblica Inc.

King James Version.

ABOUT *the* AUTHOR

As a child, Dr. Avis Sparks loved story time with her mother. Avis enjoyed listening and imagining the Bible stories that her mother told so animatedly. The stories of Daniel in the lion's den and David and Goliath excited her. She could feel the boldness and faith that the characters had in God and wanted the same relationship with Him. Her love for a good story transformed into a passion for the Word of God, and as she grew, she truly began to understand the love that God had for her. When she was young, her mother encouraged her to study God's Word and know it for herself. In her efforts to do so, she grew in not only faith but also the desire to share the love and Word of God with others. Her shyness kept her from starting many conversations, but her passion drove her to write personal letters instead. Her writing progressed to journaling and writing sermonettes, poetry, inspirational devotionals, and books.

Avis spent most of her higher-learning experience in the sciences. She received a BS in biology from Tougaloo College and a PhD in biomedical sciences from the University of Arkansas for medical sciences. After finishing postdoctoral training at the Children's Hospital of New Orleans, Avis had the opportunity to stay home with her children, dedicate time to studying the Word of God, and finally write the books she felt inspired to share. She truly believes that the Word of God and His love addresses all the issues of humanity, and she wants to share the truths she has learned with others.

In addition to God blessing her with love for a good story, science, and writing, Avis is a wife, a mother of two, a budding author, a teacher, a speaker, and the founder of A Spark Ministries LLC. Find out more about Avis and A Spark Ministries at *Asparkministries.com*

CPSIA information can be obtained
at www.ICGtesting.com
Printed in the USA
LVHW081932141120
671501LV00008B/104